CEH™
Official
Certified Ethical Hacker
Review Guide

CEH™
Official
Certified Ethical Hacker
Review Guide

Kimberly Graves

BICENTENNIAL
1807
WILEY
2007
BICENTENNIAL

Wiley Publishing, Inc.

Acquisitions and Development Editor: Jeff Kellum
Technical Editor: Sondra Schneider
Production Editor: Rachel Meyers
Copy Editor: Tiffany Taylor
Production Manager: Tim Tate
Vice President and Executive Group Publisher: Richard Swadley
Vice President and Executive Publisher: Joseph B. Wikert
Vice President and Publisher: Neil Edde
Media Project Supervisor: Laura Atkinson
Media Development Specialist: Steve Kudirka
Media Quality Assurance: Angie Denny
Book Designers: Judy Fung and Bill Gibson
Compositor: Craig Woods, Happenstance Type-O-Rama
Proofreader: Nancy Riddiough
Indexer: Ted Laux
Anniversary Logo Design: Richard Pacifico
Cover Designer: Ryan Sneed
Copyright © 2007 by Wiley Publishing, Inc., Indianapolis, Indiana
Published simultaneously in Canada
ISBN-13: 978-0-7821-4437-6

For general information on our other products and services or to obtain technical support, please contact our Customer Care Department within the U.S. at (800) 762-2974, outside the U.S. at (317) 572-3993 or fax (317) 572-4002.

Wiley also publishes its books in a variety of electronic formats. Some content that appears in print may not be available in electronic books.

Library of Congress Cataloging-in-Publication Data.
Graves, Kimberly, 1974-
  CEH : certified ethical hacker review guide / Kimberly Graves.
     p. cm.
  ISBN-13: 978-0-7821-4437-6 (paper/cd-rom)
  ISBN-10: 0-7821-4437-3 (paper/cd-rom)
 1. Electronic data processing personnel--Certification. 2. Computer security--Examinations--Study guides. 3. Computer hackers. I. Title.
  QA76.3.G69 2007
  005.8--dc22
                        2006101131

10 9 8 7 6 5 4 3 2

Contents at a Glance

Contents

Introduction

The Certified Ethical Hacker (CEH) exam was developed by the International Council of E-Commerce Consultants (EC-Council) to provide an industry-wide means of certifying the competency of security professionals. The CEH certification is granted to those who have attained the level of knowledge and troubleshooting skills needed to provide capable support in the field of computer and network security.

The CEH exam is periodically updated to keep the certification applicable to the most recent hardware and software. This is necessary because a CEH must be able to work on the latest equipment. The most recent revisions to the objectives—and to the whole program—were enacted in 2006 and are reflected in this book.

What Is CEH Certification?

The CEH certification was created to offer a wide-ranging certification, in the sense that it's intended to certify competence with many different makers/vendors. This certification is designed for security officers, auditors, security professionals, site administrators, and anyone who deals with the security of the network infrastructure on a day-to-day basis.

The goal of ethical hackers is to help organizations take preemptive measures against malicious attacks by attacking systems themselves, all the while staying within legal limits. This philosophy stems from the proven practice of trying to catch a thief by thinking like a thief. As technology advances organizations increasingly depend on technology, and information assets have evolved into critical components of survival.

You need to pass only a single exam to become a CEH. But obtaining this certification doesn't mean you can provide services to a company—this is just the first step. By obtaining your CEH certification, you'll be able to obtain more experience, build on your interest in networks, and subsequently pursue more complex and in-depth network knowledge and certifications.

For the latest exam pricing and updates to the registration procedures, call either Thomson Prometric at (866) 776-6387 or (800) 776-4276, or Pearson VUE at (877) 680-3926. You can also go to either www.2test.com or www.prometric.com (for Thomson Prometric) or www.vue.com (for Pearson VUE) for additional information or to register online. If you have further questions about the scope of the exams or related EC-Council programs, refer to the EC-Council website at www.eccouncil.org.

Who Should Buy This Book?

CEH: Official Certified Ethical Hacker Review Guide is designed to be a succinct, portable exam review guide that can be used either in conjunction with a more complete study program, computer-based training courseware, or classroom/lab environment, or as an exam review tool for those want to brush up before taking the exam. It isn't our goal to give away the answers, but rather to identify those topics on which you can expect to be tested.

If you want to become a CEH, this book is definitely what you need. However, if you just want to attempt to pass the exam without really understanding the basics of ethical hacking, this guide isn't for you. It's written for people who want to create a foundation of the skills and knowledge necessary to pass the exam, and then take what they learned and apply it to the real world.

How to Use This Book and the CD

We've included several testing features in the book and on the CD-ROM. These tools will help you retain vital exam content as well as prepare to sit for the actual exam:

Chapter Review Questions   To test your knowledge as you progress through the book, there are review questions at the end of each chapter. As you finish each chapter, answer the review questions and then check your answers—the correct answers appear on the page following the last review question. You can go back to reread the section that deals with each question you got wrong to ensure that you answer correctly the next time you're tested on the material.

Electronic Flashcards   You'll find flashcard questions on the CD for on-the-go review. These are short questions and answers, just like the flashcards you probably used to study in school. You can answer them on your PC or download them onto a Palm device for quick and convenient reviewing.

Test Engine   The CD also contains the Sybex Test Engine. Using this custom test engine, you can identify weak areas up front and then develop a solid studying strategy using each of these robust testing features. Our thorough readme file will walk you through the quick, easy installation process.

In addition to taking the chapter review questions, you'll find sample exams. Take these practice exams just as if you were taking the actual exam (without any reference material). When you've finished the first exam, move on to the next one to solidify your test-taking skills. If you get more than 90 percent of the answers correct, you're ready to take the certification exam.

Glossary of Terms in PDF   The CD-ROM contains a useful Glossary of Terms in PDF (Adobe Acrobat) format so you can easily read it on any computer. If you have to travel and brush up on any key terms, and you have a laptop with a CD-ROM drive, you can do so with this resource.

Tips for Taking the CEH Exam

Here are some general tips for taking your exam successfully:

- Bring two forms of ID with you. One must be a photo ID, such as a driver's license. The other can be a major credit card or a passport. Both forms must include a signature.

- Arrive early at the exam center so you can relax and review your study materials, particularly tables and lists of exam-related information.

- Read the questions carefully. Don't be tempted to jump to an early conclusion. Make sure you know exactly what the question is asking.

- Don't leave any unanswered questions. Unanswered questions are scored against you.

- There will be questions with multiple correct responses. When there is more than one correct answer, a message at the bottom of the screen will prompt you to either "Choose two" or "Choose all that apply." Be sure to read the messages displayed to know how many correct answers you must choose.

- When answering multiple-choice questions you're not sure about, use a process of elimination to get rid of the obviously incorrect answers first. Doing so will improve your odds if you need to make an educated guess.

- On form-based tests (non-adaptive), because the hard questions will eat up the most time, save them for last. You can move forward and backward through the exam.

- For the latest pricing on the exams and updates to the registration procedures, visit EC-Council's website at www.eccouncil.org.

The CEH Exam Objectives

At the beginning of each chapter in this book, we have included the complete listing of the CEH objectives as they appear on EC-Council's website. These are provided for easy reference and to assure you that you are on track with the objectives.

 Exam objectives are subject to change at any time without prior notice and at EC-Council's sole discretion. Please visit the CEH Certification page of EC-Council's website (www.eccouncil.org/312-50.htm) for the most current listing of exam objectives.

Ethics and Legality

- Understand ethical hacking terminology.
- Define the job role of an ethical hacker.
- Understand the different phases involved in ethical hacking.
- Identify different types of hacking technologies.
- List the five stages of ethical hacking.
- What is hacktivism?
- List different types of hacker classes.
- Define the skills required to become an ethical hacker.
- What is vulnerability research?
- Describe the ways of conducting ethical hacking.
- Understand the legal implications of hacking.
- Understand 18 U.S.C. § 1030 US Federal Law.

Footprinting

- Define the term footprinting.
- Describe information gathering methodology.
- Describe competitive intelligence.
- Understand DNS enumeration.
- Understand Whois, ARIN lookup.
- Identify different types of DNS records.
- Understand how traceroute is used in footprinting.
- Understand how e-mail tracking works.
- Understand how web spiders work.

Scanning

- Define the terms port scanning, network scanning, and vulnerability scanning.
- Understand the CEH scanning methodology.
- Understand ping sweep techniques.
- Understand nmap command switches.
- Understand SYN, stealth, XMAS, NULL, IDLE and FIN scans.
- List TCP communication flag types.
- Understand war dialing techniques.
- Understand banner grabbing and OF fingerprinting techniques.
- Understand how proxy servers are used in launching an attack.
- How does anonymizers work?
- Understand HTTP tunneling techniques.
- Understand IP spoofing techniques.

Enumeration

- What is enumeration?
- What is meant by null sessions?
- What is SNMP enumeration?
- What are the steps involved in performing enumeration?

System Hacking

- Understanding password cracking techniques.
- Understanding different types of passwords.
- Identify various password cracking tools.

- Understand escalating privileges.
- Understanding keyloggers and other spyware technologies.
- Understand how to hide files.
- Understand rootkits.
- Understand steganography technologies.
- Understand how to covering your tracks and erase evidence.

Trojans and Backdoors

- What is a Trojan?
- What is meant by overt and covert channels?
- List the different types of Trojans.
- What are the indications of a Trojan attack?
- Understand how Netcat Trojan works.
- What is meant by wrapping?
- How do reverse connecting Trojans work?
- What are the countermeasure techniques in preventing Trojans?
- Understand Trojan evading techniques.

Sniffers

- Understand the protocols susceptible to sniffing.
- Understand active and passive sniffing.
- Understand ARP poisoning.
- Understand ethereal capture and display filters.
- Understand MAC flooding.
- Understand DNS spoofing techniques.
- Describe sniffing countermeasures.

Denial of Service

- Understand the types of DoS attacks.
- Understand how a DDoS attack works.
- Understand how BOT s/BOTNETs work.
- What is smurf attack?
- What is SYN flooding?
- Describe the DoS/DDoS countermeasures .

Social Engineering

- What is social engineering?
- What are the common types of attacks?
- Understand dumpster diving.
- Understand reverse social engineering.
- Understand insider attacks.
- Understand identity theft.
- Describe phishing attacks.
- Understand online scams.
- Understand URL obfuscation.
- Social engineering countermeasures.

Session Hijacking

- Understand spoofing vs. hijacking.
- List the types of session hijacking.
- Understand sequence prediction.
- What are the steps in performing session hijacking?
- Describe how you would prevent session hijacking.

Hacking Web Servers

- List the types of web server vulnerabilities.
- Understand the attacks against web servers.
- Understand IIS Unicode exploits.
- Understand patch management techniques.
- Understand Web Application Scanner.
- What is Metasploit Framework?
- Describe web server hardening methods.

Web Application Vulnerabilities

- Understand how web application works.
- Objectives of web application hacking.
- Anatomy of an attack.
- Web application threats.
- Understand Google hacking.
- Understand web application countermeasures.

Web-Based Password-Cracking Techniques

- List the authentication types
- What is a password cracker?
- How does a password cracker work?
- Understand password attacks—classification
- Understand password cracking countermeasures

SQL Injection

- What is SQL injection?
- Understand the steps to conduct SQL injection.
- Understand SQL Server vulnerabilities.
- Describe SQL injection countermeasures.

Wireless Hacking

- Overview of WEP, WPA authentication systems and cracking techniques.
- Overview of wireless sniffers and SSID, MAC spoofing.
- Understand rogue access points.
- Understand wireless hacking techniques.
- Describe the methods in securing wireless networks.

Virus and Worms

- Understand the difference between a virus and a worm.
- Understand the types of viruses.
- How a virus spreads and infects the system.
- Understand antivirus evasion techniques.
- Understand virus detection methods.

Physical Security

- Physical security breach incidents.
- Understand physical security.
- What is the need for physical security?
- Who is accountable for physical security?
- Factors affecting physical security.

Linux Hacking

- Understand how to compile a Linux kernel.
- Understand GCC compilation commands.

- Understand how to install LKM modules.
- Understand Linux hardening methods.

Evading IDS, Honeypots, and Firewalls

- List the types of intrusion detection systems and evasion techniques.
- List firewall and honeypot evasion techniques.

Buffer Overflows

- Overview of stack based buffer overflows.
- Identify the different types of buffer overflows and methods of detection.
- Overview of buffer overflow mutation techniques.

Cryptography

- Overview of cryptography and encryption techniques.
- Describe how public and private keys are generated.
- Overview of MD5, SHA, RC4, RC5, Blowfish algorithms.

Penetration Testing Methodologies

- Overview of penetration testing methodologies.
- List the penetration testing steps.
- Overview of the Pen-Test legal framework.
- Overview of the Pen-Test deliverables.
- List the automated penetration testing tools.

How to Contact the Publisher

Sybex welcomes feedback on all of its titles. Visit the Sybex website at www.sybex.com for book updates and additional certification information. You'll also find forms you can use to submit comments or suggestions regarding this or any other Sybex title.

About the Author

Kimberly Graves has over 10 years of IT experience. She currently works with Symbol Technologies and other leading wireless and security vendors as an instructor. She has served various educational institutions in Washington, D.C., as an adjunct professor while simultaneously serving as a subject-matter expert for several certification programs such as the Certified Wireless Network Professional (CWNP) and Intel Certified Network Engineer. Recently, Kimberly has been utilizing her CWNA, Certified Wireless Security Professional (CWSP), and Certified Ethical Hacker (CEH) certificates to teach and develop course material for the Department of Veterans Affairs, the USAF, and the NSA.

CEH™
Official
Certified Ethical Hacker
Review Guide

Chapter

1

Introduction to Ethical Hacking, Ethics, and Legality

CEH EXAM OBJECTIVES COVERED IN THIS CHAPTER:

✓ Understanding Ethical Hacking Terminology

✓ Identifying Different Types of Hacking Technologies

✓ Understanding the Different Phases Involved in Ethical Hacking and Listing the Five Stages of Ethical Hacking

✓ What Is Hacktivism?

✓ Listing Different Types of Hacker Classes

✓ Defining the Skills Required to Become an Ethical Hacker

✓ What Is Vulnerability Research?

✓ Describing the Ways to Conduct Ethical Hacking

✓ Understanding the Legal Implications of Hacking

✓ Understanding 18 U.S.C. § 1029 and 1030 U.S. Federal Law

Most people think hackers have extraordinary skill and knowledge that allow them to hack into computer systems and find valuable information. The term *hacker* conjures up images of a young computer whiz who types a few commands at a computer screen—and poof! The computer spits back account numbers or other confidential data. In reality, a good hacker just has to understand how a computer system works and know what tools to employ in order to find a security weakness.

The realm of hackers and how they operate is unknown to most computer and security professionals. The goal of this chapter is to introduce you to the world of the hacker and to define the terms that will be tested on the Certified Ethical Hacker (CEH) exam.

Understanding Ethical Hacking Terminology

Being able to understand and define terminology is an important part of a CEH's responsibility. In this section, we'll discuss a number of terms you need to be familiar with.

A *threat* is an environment or situation that could lead to a potential breach of security. Ethical hackers look for and prioritize threats when performing a security analysis.

In computer security, an *exploit* is a piece of software that takes advantage of a bug, glitch, or vulnerability, leading to unauthorized access, privilege escalation, or denial of service on a computer system.

There are two methods of classifying exploits:

A *remote exploit* works over a network and exploits security vulnerabilities without any prior access to the vulnerable system.

A *local exploit* requires prior access to the vulnerable system to increase privileges.

An exploit is a defined way to breach the security of an IT system through a vulnerability.

A *vulnerability* is an existence of a software flaw, logic design, or implementation error that can lead to an unexpected and undesirable event executing bad or damaging instructions to the system.

A *target of evaluation* is a system, program, or network that is the subject of a security analysis or attack.

An *attack* occurs when a system is compromised based on a vulnerability. Many attacks are perpetuated via an exploit. Ethical hackers use tools to find systems that may be vulnerable to an exploit because of the operating system, network configuration, or applications installed on the systems, and prevent an attack. This book provides you the toolset necessary to become an ethical hacker.

In addition to knowing these terms, it's also important to identify the differences between an ethical hacker and a malicious hacker, and to understand what ethical hackers do.

Identifying Different Types of Hacking Technologies

Many methods and tools exist for locating vulnerabilities, running exploits, and compromising systems. Trojans, backdoors, sniffers, rootkits, exploits, buffer overflows, and SQL injection are all technologies that can be used to hack a system or network. These technologies and attack methods will each be discussed in later chapters. Many are so complex that an entire chapter is devoted to explaining the attack and applicable technologies.

Most hacking tools exploit weaknesses in one of the following four areas:

Operating systems   Many systems administrators install operating systems with the default settings, resulting in potential vulnerabilities that remain unpatched.

Applications   Applications usually aren't tested for vulnerabilities when developers are writing the code, which can leave many programming flaws that a hacker can exploit.

Shrink-wrap code   Many off-the-shelf programs come with extra features the common user isn't aware of, which can be used to exploit the system. One example is macros in Microsoft Word, which can allow a hacker to execute programs from within the application.

Misconfigurations   Systems can also be misconfigured or left at the lowest common security settings to increase ease of use for the user, which may result in vulnerability and an attack.

This book will cover all these technologies and hacking tools in depth in later chapters. It's necessary to understand the types of attacks and basics of security before you learn all the technologies associated with an attack.

In addition to the various types of technologies a hacker can use, there are different types of attacks. Attacks can be categorized as either *passive* or *active*. Passive and active attacks are used on both network security infrastructures and on hosts. Active attacks actually alter the system or network they're attacking, whereas passive attacks attempt to gain information from the system. Active attacks affect the availability, integrity, and authenticity of data; passive attacks are breaches of confidentiality.

In addition to the active and passive categories, attacks are categorized as either *inside* or *outside* attacks. Figure 1.1 shows the relationship between passive and active attacks, and inside and outside attacks. An attack originating from within the security perimeter of an organization is an inside attack and usually is caused by an "insider" who gains access to more resources than expected. An outside attack originates from a source outside the security perimeter, such as the Internet or a remote access connection.

FIGURE 1.1   Types of attacks

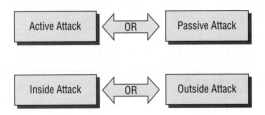

 Most network security breaches originate from within an organization—usually from the company's own employees or contractors.

Understanding the Different Phases Involved in Ethical Hacking and Listing the Five Stages of Ethical Hacking

An ethical hacker follows processes similar to those of a malicious hacker. The steps to gain and maintain entry into a computer system are similar no matter what the hacker's intentions are. Figure 1.2 illustrates the five phases that hackers generally follow in hacking a system. The following sections cover these five phases.

FIGURE 1.2   Phases of hacking

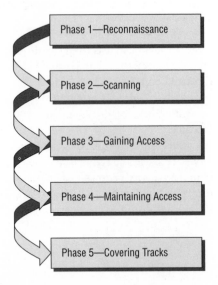

Phase 1: Passive and Active Reconnaissance

Passive reconnaissance involves gathering information regarding a potential target without the targeted individual's or company's knowledge. Passive reconnaissance can be as simple as watching a building to identify what time employees enter the building and when they leave. However, it's usually done using Internet searches or by Googling an individual or company to gain information. This process is generally called *information gathering*. Social engineering and dumpster diving are also considered passive information-gathering methods.

Sniffing the network is another means of passive reconnaissance and can yield useful information such as IP address ranges, naming conventions, hidden servers or networks, and other available services on the system or network. Sniffing network traffic is similar to building monitoring: A hacker watches the flow of data to see what time certain transactions take place and where the traffic is going.

Active reconnaissance involves probing the network to discover individual hosts, IP addresses, and services on the network. This usually involves more risk of detection than passive reconnaissance and is sometimes called *rattling the doorknobs*. Active reconnaissance can give a hacker an indication of security measures in place (is the front door locked?), but the process also increases the chance of being caught or at least raising suspicion.

Both passive and active reconnaissance can lead to the discovery of useful information to use in an attack. For example, it's usually easy to find the type of web server and the operating system (OS) version number that a company is using. This information may enable a hacker to find a vulnerability in that OS version and exploit the vulnerability to gain more access.

Phase 2: Scanning

Scanning involves taking the information discovered during reconnaissance and using it to examine the network. Tools that a hacker may employ during the scanning phase can include dialers, port scanners, network mappers, sweepers, and vulnerability scanners. Hackers are seeking any information that can help them perpetrate attack such as computer names, IP addresses, and user accounts.

The methods and tools used in scanning are discussed in detail in Chapter 3, "Scanning and Enumeration."

Phase 3: Gaining Access

This is the phase where the real hacking takes place. Vulnerabilities discovered during the reconnaissance and scanning phase are now exploited to gain access. The method of connection the hacker uses for an exploit can be a local area network (LAN, either wired or wireless), local access to a PC, the Internet, or offline. Examples include stack-based buffer overflows, denial of service (DoS), and session hijacking. These topics will be discussed in later chapters. Gaining access is known in the hacker world as *owning* the system.

Phase 4: Maintaining Access

Once a hacker has gained access, they want to keep that access for future exploitation and attacks. Sometimes, hackers *harden* the system from other hackers or security personnel by securing their exclusive access with backdoors, rootkits, and Trojans. Once the hacker owns the system, they can use it as a base to launch additional attacks. In this case, the owned system is sometimes referred to as a *zombie* system.

Phase 5: Covering Tracks

Once hackers have been able to gain and maintain access, they cover their tracks to avoid detection by security personnel, to continue to use the owned system, to remove evidence of hacking, or to avoid legal action. Hackers try to remove all traces of the attack, such as log files or intrusion detection system (IDS) alarms. Examples of activities during this phase of the attack include steganography, the use of tunneling protocols, and altering log files. Steganography and use of tunneling for purposes of hacking will be discussed in later chapters.

What Is Hacktivism?

Hacktivism refers to hacking for a cause. These hackers usually have a social or political agenda. Their intent is to send a message through their hacking activity while gaining visibility for their cause and themselves.

Many of these hackers participate in activities such as defacing websites, creating viruses, DoS, or other disruptive attacks to gain notoriety for their cause. Hacktivism commonly targets government agencies, political groups, and any other entities these groups or individuals perceive as "bad" or "wrong."

Listing Different Types of Hacker Classes

Hackers can be divided into three groups: white hats, black hats, and grey hats. Ethical hackers usually fall into the white-hat category, but sometimes they're former grey hats who have become security professionals and who use their skills in an ethical manner.

White hats   White Hats are the good guys, the ethical hackers who use their hacking skills for defensive purposes. White-hat hackers are usually security professionals with knowledge of hacking and the hacker toolset and who use this knowledge to locate weaknesses and implement countermeasures.

Black hats   Black hats are the bad guys: the malicious hackers or *crackers* who use their skills for illegal or malicious purposes. They break into or otherwise violate the system integrity of remote machines, with malicious intent. Having gained unauthorized access, black-hat hackers destroy vital data, deny legitimate users service, and basically cause problems for their targets. Black-hat hackers and crackers can easily be differentiated from white-hat hackers because their actions are malicious.

Grey hats   Grey hats are hackers who may work offensively or defensively, depending on the situation. This is the dividing line between hacker and cracker. Both are powerful forces on the Internet, and both will remain permanently. And some individuals qualify for both categories. The existence of such individuals further clouds the division between these two groups of people.

In addition to these groups, there are self-proclaimed ethical hackers, who are interested in hacker tools mostly from a curiosity standpoint. They may want to highlight security problems in a system or educate victims so they secure their systems properly. These hackers are doing their "victims" a favor. For instance, if a weakness is discovered in a service offered by an investment bank, the hacker is doing the bank a favor by giving the bank a chance to rectify the vulnerability.

From a more controversial point of view, some people consider the act of hacking itself to be unethical, like breaking and entering. But the belief that "ethical" hacking excludes destruction at least moderates the behavior of people who see themselves as "benign" hackers. According to this view, it may be one of the highest forms of hackerly courtesy to break into a system and then explain to the system operator exactly how it was done and how the hole can be plugged; the hacker is acting as an unpaid—and unsolicited—*tiger team* (a group that conducts security audits for hire). This approach has gotten many ethical hackers in legal trouble. Make sure you know the law and your legal liabilities when engaging in ethical hacking activity.

Many self-proclaimed ethical hackers are trying to break into the security field as consultants. Most companies don't look favorably on someone who appears on their doorstep with confidential data and offers to "fix" the security holes "for a price." Responses range from "thank you for this information, we'll fix the problem" to calling the police to arrest the self-proclaimed ethical hacker.

Being able to identify the types of hackers is important, but determining the differences is equally—if not more—important. We'll look at this in the following sections.

Ethical Hackers and Crackers—Who Are They?

Many people ask, "Can hacking be ethical?" Yes! Ethical hackers are usually security professionals or network penetration testers who use their hacking skills and toolsets for defensive and protective purposes. Ethical hackers who are security professionals test their network and systems security for vulnerabilities using the same tools that a hacker might use to compromise the network. Any computer professional can learn the skills of ethical hacking.

As we mentioned earlier, the term *cracker* describes a hacker who uses their hacking skills and toolset for destructive or offensive purposes such as disseminating viruses or performing DoS attacks to compromise or bring down systems and networks. No longer just looking for fun, these hackers are sometimes paid to damage corporate reputations or steal or reveal credit-card information, while slowing business processes and compromising the integrity of the organization.

 Another name for a cracker is a *malicious hacker*.

What Do Ethical Hackers Do?

Ethical hackers are motivated by different reasons, but their purpose is usually the same as that of crackers: They're trying to determine what an intruder can see on a targeted network or system, and what the hacker can do with that information. This process of testing the security of a system or network is known as a *penetration test.*

Hackers break into computer systems. Contrary to widespread myth, doing this doesn't usually involve a mysterious leap of hackerly brilliance, but rather persistence and the dogged repetition of a handful of fairly well-known tricks that exploit common weaknesses in the security of target systems. Accordingly, most crackers are only mediocre hackers.

Many ethical hackers detect malicious hacker activity as part of the security team of an organization tasked with defending against malicious hacking activity. When hired, an ethical hacker asks the organization what is to be protected, from whom, and what resources the company is willing to expend in order to gain protection.

Goals Attackers Try to Achieve

Security consists of four basic elements:

- Confidentiality
- Authenticity
- Integrity
- Availability

A hacker's goal is to exploit vulnerabilities in a system or network to find a weakness in one or more of the four elements of security. In performing a DoS attack, a hacker attacks the availability elements of systems and networks. Although a DoS attack can take many forms, the main purpose is to use up system resources or bandwidth. A flood of incoming messages to the target system essentially forces it to shut down, thereby denying service to legitimate users of the system. Although the media focuses on the target of DoS attacks, in reality such attacks have many victims—the final target and the systems the intruder controls.

Information theft, such as stealing passwords or other data as it travels in cleartext across trusted networks, is a confidentiality attack, because it allows someone other than the intended recipient to gain access to the data. This theft isn't limited to data on network servers. Laptops, disks, and backup tapes are all at risk. These company-owned devices are loaded with confidential information and can give a hacker information about the security measures in place at an organization.

Bit-flipping attacks are considered integrity attacks because the data may have been tampered with in transit or at rest on computer systems; therefore system administrators are unable to verify the data is as it the sender intended it. A bit-flipping attack is an attack on a cryptographic cipher: The attacker changes the ciphertext in such as a way as to result in a predictable change of the plaintext, although the attacker doesn't learn the plaintext itself. This type of attack isn't directly against the cipher but against a message or series of messages. In the extreme, this can become a DoS attack against all messages on a particular channel using that cipher. The attack is especially dangerous when the attacker knows the format of the message. When a bit-flipping attack is applied to digital signatures, the attacker may be able to change a promissory note stating "I owe you $10.00" into one stating "I owe you $10,000."

MAC address spoofing is an authentication attacks because it allows an unauthorized device to connect to the network when MAC filtering is in place, such as on a wireless network. By spoofing the MAC address of a legitimate wireless station, an intruder can take on that station's identity and use the network.

Security, Functionality, and Ease of Use Triangle

As a security professional, it's difficult to strike a balance between adding security barriers to prevent an attack and allowing the system to remain functional for users. The security, functionality, and ease of use triangle is a representation of the balance between security and functionality and the system's ease of use for users (see Figure 1.3). In general, as security increases, the system's functionality and ease of use decrease for users.

FIGURE 1.3   Security, functionality, and ease of use triangle

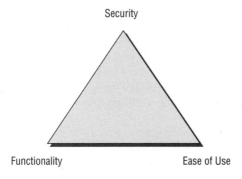

In an ideal world, security professionals would like to have the highest level of security on all systems; however, sometimes this isn't possible. Too many security barriers make it difficult for users to use the system and impede the system's functionality. Suppose that in order to gain entry to your office at work, you had to first pass through a guard checkpoint at the entrance to the parking lot to verify your license plate number, then show a badge as you entered the building, then use a passcode to gain entry to the elevator, and finally use a key to unlock your office door. You might feel the security checks were too stringent! Any one of those checks could cause you to be detained and consequently miss an important meeting—for example, if your car was in the repair shop and you had a rental car, or you forgot your key or badge to access the building, elevator, or office door.

Defining the Skills Required to Become an Ethical Hacker

Ethical hackers who stay a step ahead of malicious hackers must be computer systems experts who are very knowledgeable about computer programming, networking and operating systems. In-depth knowledge about highly targeted platforms (such as Windows, Unix, and Linux) is also a requirement. Patience, persistence, and immense perseverance are important qualities that many hackers possess because of the length of time and level of concentration required for most attacks/compromises to pay off.

Most ethical hackers are knowledgeable about security areas and related issues but don't necessarily have a strong command of the countermeasure that can prevent attacks. The following chapters of this book will address both the vulnerabilities and the countermeasures to prevent certain types of attacks.

What Is Vulnerability Research?

Vulnerability research is the process of discovering vulnerabilities and design weaknesses that could lead to an attack on a system. Several websites and tools exist to aid the ethical hacker in maintaining a current list of vulnerabilities and possible exploits for their systems or networks. It's essential that a systems administrator keep current on the latest viruses, Trojans, and other common exploits in order to adequately protect their systems and network. Also, by becoming familiar with the newest threats, an administrator can learn how to detect, prevent, and recover from an attack.

Describing the Ways to Conduct Ethical Hacking

Ethical hacking is usually conducted in a structured and organized manner, usually as part of a penetration test or security audit. The depth and breadth of the systems and applications to be tested are usually determined by the needs and concerns of the client. Many ethical hackers are members of a tiger team.

The following steps are a framework for performing a security audit of an organization:

1. Talk to the client, and discuss the needs to be addressed during the testing.

2. Prepare and sign nondisclosure agreement (NDA) documents with the client.

3. Organize an ethical hacking team, and prepare a schedule for testing.

4. Conduct the test.

5. Analyze the results of the testing, and prepare a report.

6. Present the report to the client.

 In-depth penetration testing and security auditing information is discussed in EC-Council's Licensed Penetration Tester (LPT) certification.

Creating a Security Evaluation Plan

Many ethical hackers acting in the role of security professionals use their skills to perform security evaluations or penetration tests. These tests and evaluations have three phases, generally ordered as follows:

The Preparation phase involves a formal agreement between the ethical hacker and the organization. This agreement should include the full scope of the test, the types of attacks (inside or outside) to be used, and the testing types: white, black, or grey box. (These types are defined later, in the section "Testing Types.")

During the Conduct Security Evaluation phase, the tests are conducted, after which the tester prepares a formal report of vulnerabilities and other findings. The findings are presented to the organization in the Conclusion phase along with any recommendations to improve security.

Types of Ethical Hacks

Ethical hackers can use many different methods to breach an organization's security during a simulated attack or penetration test. The most common methods follow:

Remote network   A remote network hack attempts to simulate an intruder launching an attack over the Internet. The ethical hacker tries to break or find a vulnerability in the outside defenses of the network, such as firewall, proxy, or router vulnerabilities.

Remote dial-up network   A remote dial-up network hack tries to simulate an intruder launching an attack against the client's modem pools. *War dialing* is the process of repetitive dialing to find an open system and is an example of such an attack.

Local network   A local network hack simulates someone with physical access gaining additional unauthorized access using the local network. The ethical hacker must gain direct access to the local network in order to launch this type of attack.

Stolen equipment   A stolen-equipment hack simulates theft of a critical information resource such as a laptop owned by an employee. Information such as usernames, passwords, security settings, and encryption types can be gained by stealing a laptop.

Social engineering   A social-engineering attack checks the integrity of the organization's employees by using the telephone or face-to-face communication to gather information for use in an attack. Social engineering attacks can be used to acquire usernames, passwords, or other organizational security measures.

Physical entry   A physical-entry attack attempts to compromise the organization's physical premises. An ethical hacker who gains physical access can plant viruses, Trojans, rootkits, or hardware key loggers (physical device used to record keystrokes) directly on systems in the target network.

Testing Types

When performing a security test or penetration test, an ethical hacker utilizes one or more types of testing on the system. Each type simulates an attacker with different levels of knowledge about the target organization. These types are as follows:

Black box   Black-box testing involves performing a security evaluation and testing with no prior knowledge of the network infrastructure or system to be tested. Testing simulates an attack by a malicious hacker outside the organization's security perimeter.

White box   White-box testing involves performing a security evaluation and testing with complete knowledge of the network infrastructure such as a network administrator would have.

Grey box   Grey-box testing involves performing a security evaluation and testing internally. Testing examines the extent of access by insiders within the network.

Ethical Hacking Report

The result of a network penetration test or security audit is an ethical hacking report. This report details the results of the hacking activity, the types of tests performed, and the hacking methods used. These results are compared against the work scheduled prior to the Conduct Security Evaluation phase. Any vulnerabilities identified are detailed, and countermeasures are suggested. This document is usually delivered to the organization in hard-copy format, for security reasons.

The details of the ethical hacking report must be kept confidential, because they highlight the organization's security risks and vulnerabilities. If this document falls into the wrong hands, the results could be disastrous for the organization.

Understanding the Legal Implications of Hacking

An ethical hacker should know the penalties of unauthorized hacking into a system. No ethical hacking activities associated with a network-penetration test or security audit should begin until a signed legal document giving the ethical hacker express permission to perform the hacking activities is received from the target organization. Ethical hackers need to be judicious with their hacking skills and recognize the consequences of misusing those skills.

Computer crimes can be broadly categorized into two categories: crimes facilitated by a computer and crimes where the computer is the target.

The two most important U.S. laws regarding computer crimes are described in the following section. Although the CEH exam is international in scope, make sure you familiarize yourself with these two U.S. statutes and the punishment for hacking. Remember, intent doesn't make a hacker above the law; even an ethical hacker can be prosecuted for breaking these laws.

The Cyber Security Enhancement Act of 2002 mandates life sentences for hackers who "recklessly" endanger the lives of others. Malicious hackers who create a life-threatening situation by attacking computer networks for transportation systems, power companies, or other public services or utilities can be prosecuted under this law.

Understanding 18 U.S.C. § 1029 and 1030 U.S. Federal Law

The U.S. Code categorizes and defines the laws of the United States by titles. Title 18 details "Crimes and Criminal Procedure." Section 1029, "Fraud and related activity in connection with access devices," states that if you produce, sell, or use counterfeit access devices or telecommunications instruments with intent to commit fraud and obtain services or products with a value or $1,000, you have broken the law. Section 1029 criminalizes the misuse of computer passwords and other access devices such as token cards.

Section 1030, "Fraud and related activity in connection with computers," prohibits accessing protected computers without permission and causing damage. This statute criminalizes the spreading of viruses and worms and breaking into computer systems by unauthorized individuals.

> **NOTE** The full text of the Section 1029 and 1030 laws is included as an appendix in this book for your reference.

Exam Essentials

Understand essential hacker terminology.   Make sure you're familiar with and can define the terms *threat*, *exploit*, *vulnerability*, *target of evaluation*, and *attack*.

Understand the difference between ethical hackers and crackers.   Ethical hackers are security professionals who act defensively. Crackers are malicious hackers who choose to inflict damage on a target system.

Know the classes of hackers.   It's critical to know the differences among black-hat, white-hat, and grey-hat hackers for the exam. Know who the good guys are and who the bad guys are in the world of hacking.

Know the phases of hacking.   Passive and active reconnaissance, scanning, gaining access, maintaining access, and covering tracks are the five phases of hacking. Know the order of the phases and what happens during each phase.

Be aware of the types of attacks.   Understand the differences between active and passive and inside and outside attacks. The ability to be detected is the difference between active and passive attacks. The location of the attacker is the difference between inside and outside attacks.

Know the ethical hacking types.   Hackers can attack the network from a remote network, a remote dial-up network, or a local network, or through social engineering, stolen equipment, or physical access.

Understand the security testing types   Ethical hackers can test a network using black-box, white-box, or grey-box testing techniques.

Know the contents of an ethical hacking report.   An ethical hacking report contains information on the hacking activities performed, network or system vulnerabilities discovered, and countermeasures that should be implemented.

Know the legal implications involved in hacking.   The Cyber Security Enhancement Act of 2002 can be used to prosecute ethical hackers who recklessly endanger the lives of others.

Be aware of the laws and punishment applicable to computer intrusion.   Title 18 sections 1029 and 1030 of the U.S. Code carry strict penalties for hacking, no matter what the intent.

Review Questions

1. Which of the following statements best describes a white-hat hacker?

   A. Security professional

   B. Former black hat

   C. Former grey hat

   D. Malicious hacker

2. A security audit performed on the internal network of an organization by the network admin-istration is also known as _____.

   A. Grey-box testing

   B. Black-box testing

   C. White-box testing

   D. Active testing

   E. Passive testing

3. What is the first phase of hacking?

   A. Attack

   B. Maintaining access

   C. Gaining access

   D. Reconnaissance

   E. Scanning

4. What type of ethical hack tests access to the physical infrastructure?

   A. Internal network

   B. Remote network

   C. External network

   D. Physical access

5. The security, functionality, and ease of use triangle illustrates which concept?

   A. As security increases, functionality and ease of use increase.

   B. As security decreases, functionality and ease of use increase.

   C. As security decreases, functionality and ease of use decrease.

   D. Security does not affect functionality and ease of use.

6. Which type of hacker represents the highest risk to your network?

    A. Disgruntled employees

    B. Black-hat hackers

    C. Grey-hat hackers

    D. Script kiddies

7. What are the three phases of a security evaluation plan? (Choose three answers.)

    A. Conduct Security Evaluation

    B. Preparation

    C. Conclusion

    D. Final

    E. Reconnaissance

    F. Design Security

    G. Vulnerability Assessment

8. Hacking for a cause is called _____.

    A. Active hacking

    B. Hacktivism

    C. Activism

    D. Black-hat hacking

9. Which federal law is most commonly used to prosecute hackers?

    A. Title 12

    B. Title 18

    C. Title 20

    D. Title 2

10. When a hacker attempts to attack a host via the Internet it is known as what type of attack?

    A. Remote attack

    B. Physical access

    C. Local access

    D. Internal attack

Answers to Review Questions

1. A. Explanation: A white-hat hacker is a "good" guy who uses his skills for defensive purposes.

2. C. Explanation: White-box testing is a security audit performed with internal knowledge of the systems.

3. D. Explanation: Reconnaissance is gathering information necessary to perform the attack.

4. D. Explanation: Physical access tests access to the physical infrastructure.

5. B. Explanation: As security increases it makes it more difficult to use and less functional.

6. A. Explanation: Disgruntled employees have information which can allow them to launch a powerful attack.

7. A, B, C. Explanation: The three phases of a security evaluation plan are preparation, conduct security evaluation, and conclusion.

8. B. Explanation: Hacktivism is performed by individual who claim to be hacking for a political or social cause.

9. B. Explanation: Title 18 of the U.S. Code of law is most commonly used to prosecute hackers

10. A. Explanation: An attack from the Internet is known as a remote attack.

Chapter

2

Footprinting and Social Engineering

CEH EXAM OBJECTIVES COVERED IN THIS CHAPTER:

✓ **Footprinting**

- Define the Term Footprinting
- Describe Information Gathering Methodology
- Describe Competitive Intelligence
- Understand DNS Enumeration
- Understand Whois and ARIN Lookup
- Identify Different Types of DNS Records
- Understand How Traceroute Is Used in Footprinting
- Understand How E-Mail Tracking Works
- Understand How Web Spiders Work

✓ **Social Engineering**

- What Is Social Engineering?
- What Are the Common Types of Attacks?
- Understand Dumpster Diving
- Understand Reverse Social Engineering
- Understand Insider attacks
- Understand Identity Theft
- Describe Phishing Attacks
- Understand Online Scams
- Understand URL Obfuscation
- Social Engineering Countermeasures

This chapter addresses the first part of the hacking process, which involves information gathering or footprinting. Footprinting is the process of gathering all available information about an organization. This information can then be used later in the hacking process. Sometimes the information can be used to launch a social engineering attack. In the alternative social engineering can be used to obtain more information about an organization, which can ultimately lead to an attack.

In this chapter, we'll look at both of these hacking methods in detail and cover the most important topics you as a CEH should be familiar with.

Footprinting

Footprinting is part of the preparatory pre-attack phase and involves accumulating data regarding a target's environment and architecture, usually for the purpose of finding ways to intrude into that environment. Footprinting can reveal system vulnerabilities and identify the ease with which they can be exploited. This is the easiest way for hackers to gather information about computer systems and the companies they belong to. The purpose of this preparatory phase is to learn as much as you can about a system, its remote access capabilities, its ports and services, and any specific aspects of its security.

Define the Term Footprinting

Footprinting is defined as the process of creating a blueprint or map of an organization's network and systems. Information gathering is also known as footprinting an organization. Footprinting begins by determining the target system, application, or physical location of the target. Once this information is known, specific information about the organization is gathered using nonintrusive methods. For example, the organization's own web page may provide a personnel directory or a list of employee bios, which may prove useful if the hacker needs to use a social engineering attack to reach the objective.

A hacker may also do a Google search or a Yahoo! People search to locate information about employees.

The Google search engine can be used in creative ways to perform information gathering. The use of the Google search engine to retrieve information has been termed Google hacking. `http://groups.google.com` can be used to search the Google newsgroups. The following commands can be used to have the Google search engine perform Google hacking:

- `site` searches a specific website or domain. The website to search must be supplied after the colon.

- `filetype` searches only within the text of a particular type of file. The file type to search must be supplied after the colon. Don't include a period before the file extension.
- `link` searches within hyperlinks for a search term and identifies linked pages
- `cache` identifies the version of a web page. The URL of the site must be supplied after the colon.
- `intitle` searches for a term within the title of a document.
- `inurl` searches only within the URL (web address) of a document. The search term must follow the colon.

For example a hacker could use the following command `INURL:["parameter="]` with `FILETYPE:[ext]` and `INURL:[scriptname]` to locate certain types of vulnerable web applications.

Or a hacker could use the search string `intitle: "BorderManager information alert"` to look for Novell BorderManager Proxy/Firewall servers.

Blogs, newsgroups, and press releases are also good places to find information about the company or employees. Corporate job postings can provide information as to the type of servers or infrastructure devices a company may be using on its network.

Other information obtained may include identification of the Internet technologies being used, the operating system and hardware being used, active IP addresses, e-mail addresses and phone numbers, and corporate policies and procedures.

Generally, a hacker spends 90 percent of the time profiling and gathering information on a target and 10 percent of the time launching the attack.

Describe the Information Gathering Methodology

Information gathering can be broken into seven logical steps (see Figure 2.1). The footprinting process is performed during the first two steps of unearthing initial information and locating the network range.

The other information-gathering steps are covered in Chapter 3, "Scanning and Enumeration."

Some of the common sources used for information gathering include the following:

- Domain name lookup
- Whois
- Nslookup
- Sam Spade

FIGURE 2.1   Seven steps of information gathering

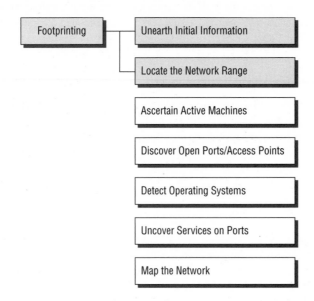

Before we discuss these tools, keep in mind that open source information can also yield a wealth of information about a target, such as phone numbers and addresses. Performing Whois requests, searching Domain Name System (DNS) tables, and scanning IP addresses for open ports are other forms of open source footprinting. Most of this information is fairly easy to get and legal to obtain.

The details of how the DNS operates and the specifics of interpreting DNS records are outside the scope of this book and won't be discussed in detail. Only the most important details as related specifically to information gathering are covered in this book. It's recommended that all CEH candidates have a thorough understanding of DNS and how name resolution works on the Internet.

Hacking Tool

Sam Spade (http://www.samspade.org) is a website that contains a collection of tools such as Whois, nslookup, and traceroute. Because they are located on a website, these tools work for any operating system and are a single location for providing information about a target organization.

Describe Competitive Intelligence

Competitive intelligence means information gathering about competitors' products, marketing, and technologies. Most competitive intelligence is nonintrusive to the company being investigated and is benign in nature—it's used for product comparison or as a sales and marketing tactic to better understand how competitors are positioning their products or services. Several tools exist for the purpose of competitive intelligence gathering and can be used by hackers to gather information about a potential target.

Understand DNS Enumeration

DNS enumeration is the process of locating all the DNS servers and their corresponding records for an organization. A company may have both internal and external DNS servers that can yield information such as usernames, computer names, and IP addresses of potential target systems.

NSlookup, DNSstuff, the American Registry for Internet Numbers (ARIN), and Whois can all be used to gain information that can then be used to perform DNS enumeration.

Nslookup and DNSstuff

One powerful tool you should be familiar with is nslookup (see Figure 2.2). This tool queries DNS servers for record information. It's included in Unix, Linux, and Windows operating systems. Hacking tools such as Sam Spade also include nslookup tools.

FIGURE 2.2   Nslookup

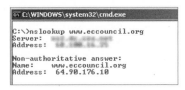

Building on the information gathered from Whois, you can use nslookup to find additional IP addresses for servers and other hosts. Using the authoritative name server information from Whois (AUTH1.NS.NYI.NET), you can discover the IP address of the mail server.

The explosion of easy-to-use tools has made hacking easy, if you know which tools to use. DNSstuff is another of those tools. Instead of using the command-line nslookup tool with its cumbersome switches to gather DNS record information, just access the website http://www.dnsstuff.com, and you can do a DNS record search online. Figure 2.3 shows a sample DNS record search on http://www.eccouncil.org using DNSstuff.com.

This search reveals all the alias records for http://www.eccouncil.org and the IP address of the web server. You can even discover all the name servers and associated IP addresses.

The exploits available to you because you have this information are discussed in Chapter 4, "System Hacking."

FIGURE 2.3   DNS record search of `http://www.eccouncil.org`

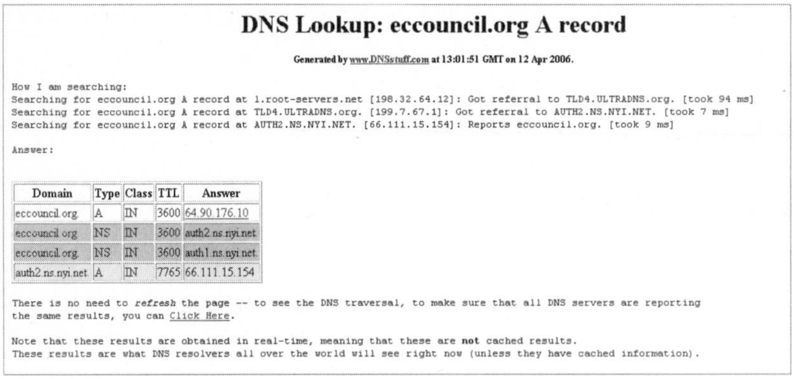

DNS Lookup: eccouncil.org A record

Generated by www.DNSstuff.com at 13:01:51 GMT on 12 Apr 2006.

How I am searching:
Searching for eccouncil.org A record at l.root-servers.net [198.32.64.12]: Got referral to TLD4.ULTRADNS.org. [took 94 ms]
Searching for eccouncil.org A record at TLD4.ULTRADNS.org. [199.7.67.1]: Got referral to AUTH2.NS.NYI.NET. [took 7 ms]
Searching for eccouncil.org A record at AUTH2.NS.NYI.NET. [66.111.15.154]: Reports eccouncil.org. [took 9 ms]

Answer:

Domain	Type	Class	TTL	Answer
eccouncil.org	A	IN	3600	64.90.176.10
eccouncil.org	NS	IN	3600	auth2.ns.nyi.net.
eccouncil.org	NS	IN	3600	auth1.ns.nyi.net.
auth2.ns.nyi.net	A	IN	7765	66.111.15.154

There is no need to *refresh* the page -- to see the DNS traversal, to make sure that all DNS servers are reporting the same results, you can Click Here.

Note that these results are obtained in real-time, meaning that these are **not** cached results.
These results are what DNS resolvers all over the world will see right now (unless they have cached information).

Understand Whois and ARIN Lookups

Whois evolved from the Unix operating system, but it can now be found in many operating systems as well as in hacking toolkits and on the Internet. This tool identifies who has registered domain names used for e-mail or websites. A uniform resource locator (URL), such as `www.Microsoft.com`, contains the domain name (`Microsoft.com`) and a host name or alias (`www`).

The Internet Corporation for Assigned Names and Numbers (ICANN) requires registration of domain names to ensure that only a single company uses a specific domain name. The Whois tool queries the registration database to retrieve contact information about the individual or organization that holds a domain registration.

Hacking Tool

Smart Whois is an information-gathering program that allows you to find all available information about an IP address, host name, or domain, including country, state or province, city, name of the network provider, administrator, and technical-support contact information. Smart Whois is a graphical version of the basic Whois program.

The ARIN is a database of information including such information as the owners of static IP addresses. The ARIN database can be queried using the Whois tool, such as the one located at `http://www.arin.net/whois`.

Figure 2.4 shows an ARIN Whois search for `http://www.yahoo.com`. Notice that addresses, e-mails, and contact information are all contained in this Whois search. This information can be used by an ethical hacker to find out who is responsible for a certain IP address and which organization owns that target system, or it can be used by a malicious hacker to perform a social engineering attack against the organization. As a security professional, you need to be aware of the information available to the public in searchable databases such as ARIN and ensure that a malicious hacker can't use this information to launch an attack against the network.

FIGURE 2.4 ARIN output for http://www.Yahoo.com

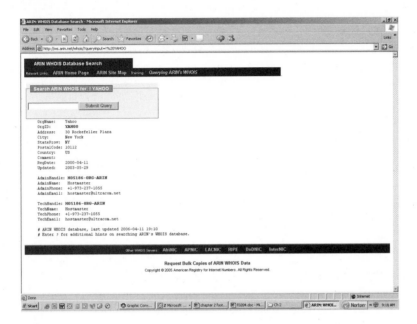

 Be aware that other geographical regions outside North American have their own Internet registries, such as RIPE NCC (Europe, the Middle East, and parts of Central Asia), LACNIC (Latin American and Caribbean Internet Addresses Registry), and APNIC (Asia Pacific Network Information Centre).

Analyzing Whois Output

A simple way to run Whois is to connect to a website (for instance, www.networksolutions.com) and conduct the Whois search. The following is the output of a Whois search of the site www.eccouncil.org:

 The contact names and server names in this book have been changed.

```
Domain ID:D81180127-LROR
Domain Name:ECCOUNCIL.ORG
Created On:14-Dec-2001 10:13:06 UTC
```

Last Updated On:19-Aug-2004 03:49:53 UTC
Expiration Date:14-Dec-2006 10:13:06 UTC
Sponsoring Registrar:Tucows Inc. (R11-LROR)
Status:OK
Registrant ID:tuTv2ItRZBMNd41A
Registrant Name: John Smith
Registrant Organization:International Council of E-Commerce Consultants
Registrant Street1:67 Wall Street, 22nd Floor
Registrant Street2:
Registrant Street3:
Registrant City:New York
Registrant State/Province:NY
Registrant Postal Code:10005-3198
Registrant Country:US
Registrant Phone:+1.2127098253
Registrant Phone Ext.:
Registrant FAX:+1.2129432300
Registrant FAX Ext.:
Registrant Email:forum@eccouncil.org
Admin ID:tus9DYvpp5mrbLNd
Admin Name: Susan Johnson
Admin Organization:International Council of E-Commerce Consultants
Admin Street1:67 Wall Street, 22nd Floor
Admin Street2:
Admin Street3:
Admin City:New York
Admin State/Province:NY
Admin Postal Code:10005-3198
Admin Country:US
Admin Phone:+1.2127098253
Admin Phone Ext.:
Admin FAX:+1.2129432300
Admin FAX Ext.:
Admin Email:ethan@eccouncil.org
Tech ID:tuE1cgAfi1VnFkpu
Tech Name:Jacob Eckel
Tech Organization:International Council of E-Commerce Consultants
Tech Street1:67 Wall Street, 22nd Floor
Tech Street2:
Tech Street3:
Tech City:New York

```
Tech State/Province:NY
Tech Postal Code:10005-3198
Tech Country:US
Tech Phone:+1.2127098253
Tech Phone Ext.:
Tech FAX:+1.2129432300
Tech FAX Ext.:
Tech Email:forum@eccouncil.org
Name Server: ns1.xyz.net
Name Server: ns2.xyz.net
```

Notice the four boldface lines. The first shows the target company or person (as well as their physical address, e-mail address, phone number, and so on). The next shows the administration or technical contact (and their contact information). The last two boldface lines show the names of domain name servers.

Finding the Address Range of the Network

Every ethical hacker needs to understand how to find the network range and subnet mask of the target system. IP addresses are used to locate, scan, and connect to target systems. You can find IP addresses in Internet registries such as ARIN or the Internet Assigned Numbers Authority (IANA).

An ethical hacker may also need to find the geographic location of the target system or network. This task can be accomplished by tracing the route a message takes as it's sent to the destination IP address. You can use tools like traceroute, VisualRoute, and NeoTrace to identify the route to the target.

Additionally, as you trace your target network, other useful information becomes available. For example, you can obtain internal IP addresses of host machines; even the Internet IP gateway of the organization may be listed. These addresses can then be used later in an attack or further scanning processes.

Identify Different Types of DNS Records

The following list describes the common DNS record types and their use:

- *A (address)*—Maps a host name to an IP address
- *SOA (Start of Authority)*—Identifies the DNS server responsible for the domain information
- *CNAME (canonical name)*—Provides additional names or aliases for the address record
- *MX (mail exchange)*—Identifies the mail server for the domain
- *SRV (service)*—Identifies services such as directory services
- *PTR (pointer)*—Maps IP addresses to host names
- *NS (name server)*—Identifies other name servers for the domain

Understand How Traceroute Is Used in Footprinting

Traceroute is a packet-tracking tool that is available for most operating systems. It operates by sending an Internet Control Message Protocol (ICMP) echo to each hop (router or gateway) along the path, until the destination address is reached. When ICMP messages are sent back from the router, the time to live (TTL) is decremented by one for each router along the path. This allows a hacker to determine how many hops a router is from the sender.

One problem with using the traceroute tool is that it times out (indicated by an asterisk) when it encounters a firewall or a packet-filtering router. Although a firewall stops the traceroute tool from discovering internal hosts on the network, it can alert an ethical hacker to the presence of a firewall; then, techniques for bypassing the firewall can be used.

These techniques are part of system hacking, which is discussed in Chapter 4: "System Hacking."

Sam Spade and many other hacking tools include a version of traceroute. The Windows operating systems use the syntax tracert *hostname* to perform a traceroute. Figure 2.5 is an example of traceroute output for a trace of www.yahoo.com.

Notice in Figure 2.5 that the message first encounters the outbound ISP to reach the Yahoo web server, and that the server's IP address is revealed as 68.142.226.42. Knowing this IP address enables the ethical hacker to perform additional scanning on that host during the scanning phase of the attack.

FIGURE 2.5   Traceroute output for www.yahoo.com

```
Select C:\WINDOWS\system32\cmd.exe

C:\>tracert www.yahoo.com

Tracing route to www.yahoo.akadns.net [68.142.226.42]
over a maximum of 30 hops:

  1     1 ms     1 ms     1 ms   192.168.1.1
  2    55 ms    32 ms    10 ms
  3    27 ms     9 ms     9 ms
  4    30 ms     9 ms     9 ms   mrfddsrj02gex070003.rd.dc.cox.net [68.100.0.149]

  5    22 ms    11 ms    11 ms   mrfdbbrj02-ge020.rd.dc.cox.net [68.1.1.6]
  6    12 ms    11 ms    12 ms   ashbbbrj01-pos020100.r2.as.cox.net [68.1.1.232]

  7    14 ms    11 ms    13 ms   68.105.30.98
  8    43 ms    12 ms    12 ms   vlan260-msr2.re1.yahoo.com [216.115.96.173]
  9    28 ms    11 ms    10 ms   t-2-1.bas2.re2.yahoo.com [206.190.33.93]
 10    28 ms    11 ms    11 ms   p11.www.re2.yahoo.com [68.142.226.42]

Trace complete.
```

Tracert identifies routers located en route to the destination's network. Because routers are generally named according to their physical location, the tracert results help you locate these devices.

Hacking Tools

NeoTrace, VisualRoute, and VisualLookout are all packet-tracking tools with a GUI or visual interface. They plot the path the packets travel on a map and can visually identify the locations of routers and other internetworking devices. These tools operate similarly to traceroute and perform the same information gathering; however, they provide a visual representation of the results.

Understand How E-Mail Tracking Works

E-mail–tracking programs allow the sender of an e-mail to know whether the recipient reads, forwards, modifies, or deletes an e-mail. Most e-mail–tracking programs work by appending a domain name to the e-mail address, such as readnotify.com. A single-pixel graphic file that isn't noticeable to the recipient is attached to the e-mail. Then, when an action is performed on the e-mail, this graphic file connects back to the server and notifies the sender of the action.

Hacking Tool

eMailTracking Pro and MailTracking.com are tools that allow an ethical hacker to track e-mail messages. When using these tools to send an e-mail, forward an e-mail, reply to an e-mail, or modify an e-mail, the resulting actions and tracks of the original e-mail are logged. The sender is notified of all actions performed on the tracked e-mail by an automatically generated e-mail.

Understand How Web Spiders Work

Spammers and anyone else interested in collecting e-mail addresses from the Internet can use *web spiders*. A web spider combs websites collecting certain information such as email addresses. The web spider uses syntax such as the @ symbol to locate email addresses then copies them into a list. These addresses are then added to a database and may be used later to send unsolicited e-mails. Web spiders can be used to locate all kinds of information on the Internet. A hacker can use a web spider to automate the information gathering process. A method to prevent web spidering of your website is to put the robots.txt file in the root of your website with a listing of directories that you want to protect from crawling.

Exam Essentials

Know how to analyze a company's infrastructure from job postings.   Search job postings from the target company or organization to determine system versions and other vital pieces of information such as firewall or IDS types and server types. Google hacking can be used to gather information from these locations, making it easy for a hacker to quickly locate information about a target.

Know how to search for a company's news, press releases, blogs, and newsgroup postings. Use all available public resources to locate information about a target company and gather data about its network and system security.

Understand how to gather information about a company's employees.   Use Yahoo! People search or other Internet search engines to find employees of the target company.

Know how to query DNS for specific record information.   Know how to use DNSstuff, nslookup, or Sam Spade to query a DNS server for record information such as hosts and IP addresses.

Understand how to perform Whois lookups for personal or company information.   Know how to use the ARIN, LACNIC, RIPE NCC, APNIC, and Whois databases to locate registrar and company contact information.

Know how to find the name of a target company's external and internal domain names. You should be able to use the Whois and Sam Spade tools to locate the domain information for a given company. Knowledge of the ARIN database is also necessary for the exam.

Know how to physically locate a target company's web server and other network infrastructure devices.   Use NeoTrace, VisualRoute, or VisualLookout to get a graphical view of the route to a target company's network. These tools enable you to physically locate the servers.

Know how to track e-mail to or from a company.   You should be able to use e-mail tracking programs to track an e-mail to a target organization and gain additional information to be used in an attack.

Social Engineering

Social engineering is a nontechnical method of breaking into a system or network. It's the process of deceiving users of a system and convincing them to give out information that can be used to defeat or bypass security mechanisms. Social engineering is important to understand because hackers can use it to attack the human element of a system and circumvent technical security measures. This method can be used to gather information before or during an attack.

What Is Social Engineering?

Social engineering is the use of influence and persuasion to deceive people for the purpose of obtaining information or persuading a victim to perform some action. A social engineer commonly uses the telephone or Internet to trick people into revealing sensitive information or to get them to do something that is against the security policies of the organization. By this method, social engineers exploit the natural tendency of a person to trust their word, rather than exploiting computer security holes. It's generally agreed that users are the weak link in security; this principle is what makes social engineering possible.

The following is an example of social engineering recounted by Kapil Raina, currently a security expert at Verisign, based on an actual workplace experience with a previous employer. "One morning a few years back, a group of strangers walked into a large shipping firm and walked out with access to the firm's entire corporate network. How did they do it? By obtaining small amounts of access, bit by bit, from a number of different employees in that firm. First, they did research about the company for two days before even attempting to set foot on the premises. For example, they learned key employees' names by calling HR. Next, they pretended to lose their key to the front door, and a man let them in. Then they "lost" their identity badges when entering the third floor secured area, smiled, and a friendly employee opened the door for them.

The strangers knew the CFO was out of town, so they were able to enter his office and obtain financial data off his unlocked computer. They dug through the corporate trash, finding all kinds of useful documents. They asked a janitor for a garbage pail in which to place their contents and carried all of this data out of the building in their hands. The strangers had studied the CFO's voice, so they were able to phone, pretending to be the CFO, in a rush, desperately in need of his network password. From there, they used regular technical hacking tools to gain super-user access into the system.

In this case, the strangers were network consultants performing a security audit for the CFO without any other employees' knowledge. They were never given any privileged information from the CFO but were able to obtain all the access they wanted through social engineering."

The most dangerous part of social engineering is that companies with authentication processes, firewalls, virtual private networks, and network-monitoring software are still wide open to attacks, because social engineering doesn't assault the security measures directly. Instead, a social-engineering attack bypasses the security measures and goes after the human element in an organization.

The Art of Manipulation

Social engineering includes the acquisition of sensitive information or inappropriate access privileges by an outsider, based on the building of inappropriate trust relationships. The goal of a social engineer is to trick someone into providing valuable information or access to that information. It preys on qualities of human nature, such as the desire to be helpful, the tendency to trust people, and the fear of getting in trouble. Hackers who are able to blend in and appear to be a part of the organization are the most successful at social-engineering attacks. This ability to blend in is commonly referred to as the *art of manipulation*.

An example of the using the art of manipulation is illustrated in the following example. The facilitator of a live Computer Security Institute demonstration showed the vulnerability of help desks when he dialed up a phone company, got transferred around, and reached the help desk. "Who's the supervisor on duty tonight?" "Oh, it's Betty." "Let me talk to Betty." [He's transferred.] "Hi Betty, having a bad day?" "No, why?…Your systems are down." She said, "my systems aren't down, we're running fine." He said, "you better sign off." She signed off. He said, "now sign on again." She signed on again. He said, "we didn't even show a blip, we show no change." He said, "sign off again." She did. "Betty, I'm going to have to sign on as you here to figure out what's happening with your ID. Let me have your user ID and password." So this senior supervisor at the help desk tells him her user ID and password. In a few minutes a hacker is able to get information that might have taken him days to get by capturing traffic and cracking the password. It is much easier to gain information by social engineering than by technical methods.

People are usually the weakest link in the security chain. A successful defense depends on having good policies in place and teaching employees to follow the policies. Social engineering is the hardest form of attack to defend against because a company can't protect itself with hardware or software alone.

What Are the Common Types Of Attacks?

Social engineering can be broken into two common types:

Human-based   Human-based social engineering refers to person-to-person interaction to retrieve the desired information. An example is calling the help desk and trying to find out a password.

Computer-based   Computer-based social engineering refers to having computer software that attempts to retrieve the desired information. An example is sending a user an e-mail and asking them to reenter a password in a web page to confirm it. This social-engineering attack is also known as *phishing*.

We'll look at each of these more closely in the following sections.

Human-Based Social Engineering

Human-based social engineering techniques can be broadly categorized as follows:

Impersonating an employee or valid user   In this type of social-engineering attack, the hacker pretends to be an employee or valid user on the system. A hacker can gain physical access by pretending to be a janitor, employee, or contractor. Once inside the facility, the hacker gathers information from trashcans, desktops, or computer systems.

Posing as an important user   In this type of attack, the hacker pretends to be an important user such as an executive or high-level manager who needs immediate assistance to gain access to a computer system or files. The hacker uses intimidation so that a lower-level employee such as a help-desk worker will assist them in gaining access to the system. Most low-level employees won't question someone who appears to be in a position of authority.

Using a third person   Using the third-person approach, a hacker pretends to have permission from an authorized source to use a system. This attack is especially effective if the supposed authorized source is on vacation or can't be contacted for verification.

Calling technical support   Calling tech support for assistance is a classic social-engineering technique. Help-desk and technical support personnel are trained to help users, which makes them good prey for social-engineering attacks.

Shoulder surfing   Shoulder surfing is a technique of gathering passwords by watching over a person's shoulder while they log in to the system. A hacker can watch a valid user log in and then use that password to gain access to the system.

Dumpster diving   Dumpster diving involves looking in the trash for information written on pieces of paper or computer printouts. The hacker can often find passwords, filenames, or other pieces of confidential information.

A more advanced method of gaining illicit information is known as *reverse social engineering*. Using this technique, a hacker creates a persona that appears to be in a position of authority so that employees ask the hacker for information, rather than the other way around. For example, a hacker can impersonate a help-desk employee and get the user to give them information such as a password.

Computer-Based Social Engineering

Computer-based social engineering attacks can include the following:

- E-mail attachments
- Fake websites
- Popup windows

 We'll look at each of these later in the chapter.

Understand Insider Attacks

If a hacker can't find any other way to hack an organization, the next best option is to infiltrate the organization by getting hired as an employee or finding a disgruntled employee to assist in the attack. Insider attacks can be powerful because employees have physical access and are able to move freely about the organization. An example might be posing as a delivery person by wearing a uniform and gaining access to a delivery room or loading dock. Another possibility to become an insider is posing as a member of the cleaning crew who has access to the inside or the building and are usually able to move about the offices. As a last resort a hacker might bribe or otherwise coerce an employee to participate in the attack by providing information such as passwords.

Understand Identity Theft

A hacker can pose as an employee or steal the employee's identity to perpetrate an attack. Information gathered in dumpster diving or shoulder surfing in combination with creating fake ID badges can gain the hacker entry into an organization. Creating a persona that can enter the building unchallenged is the goal of identity theft.

Describe Phishing Attacks

Phishing involves sending an e-mail, usually posing as a bank, credit-card company, or other financial organization. The e-mail requests that the recipient confirm banking information or reset passwords or PIN numbers. The user clicks the link in the e-mail and is redirected to a fake website. The hacker is then able to capture this information and use it for financial gain or to perpetrate other attacks. E-mails that claim the senders have a great amount of money but need your help getting it out of the country are examples of phishing attacks. These attacks prey on the common person and are aimed at getting them to provide bank account access codes or other confidential information to the hacker.

Understand Online Scams

Some websites that make free offers or other special deals can lure a victim to enter a username and password that may be the same as those they use to access their work system. The hacker can use this valid username and password once the user enters the information in the website form.

Mail attachments can be used to send malicious code to a victim's system, which could automatically execute something like a software keylogger to capture passwords. Viruses, Trojans and worms can be included in cleverly crafted e-mails to entice a victim to open the attachment. Mail attachments are considered a computer-based social engineering attack.

Here is an example of an e-mail scam which tries to convice the receiver to open an unsafe attachment:

```
Mail server report.

Our firewall determined the e-mails containing worm copies are being sent from
your computer.

Nowadays it happens from many computers, because this is a new virus type
(Network Worms).


Using the new bug in the Windows, these viruses infect the computer
unnoticeably.
After the penetrating into the computer the virus harvests all the e-mail
addresses and sends the copies of itself to these e-mail addresses

Please install updates for worm elimination and your computer restoring.

Best regards,
Customer support service
```

Pop-up windows can also be used in computer-based engineering attacks, in a similar manner to e-mail attachments. Pop-up windows with special offers or free stuff can encourage a user to unintentionally install malicious software.

Understand URL Obfuscation

URL is the Uniform Resource Locator and is commonly used in the address bar of a web browser to access a particular website. In lay terms it is the website address. URL obfuscation is the hiding or a fake URL in what appear to be a legitimate website address. For example, a website of 204.13.144.2/Citibank may appear to be a legitimate web address for Citibank but in fact is not. URL obfuscation is used in phishing attacks and some online scams to make the scam seem more legitimate. A website address may be seen as an actual financial institution name or logo, but the hyperlink leads to a fake website or IP address. When the user clicks the hyperlink, they're redirected to the hacker's site. Addresses can be obfuscated in malicious links by the use of hexadecimal or decimal notations. For example, the address 192.168.10.5 looks like 3232238085 as a decimal.
Explanation:

3232238085
The same address looks like C0A80A05 in IP hex. This conversion requires that you divide 3232238085 by 16 multiple times. Each time the remainder reveals the address, starting from the least significant value.
Explanation: 3232238085/16 = 202014880.3125 (.3125 * 16 = 5)
                202014880/16 = 12625930.0 (.0 * 16 = 0)
                12625930/16 = 789120.625 (.625 * 16 = 10 = A)
                789120/16 = 49320.0 (.0 * 16 = 0)
                49320.0/16 = 3082.5 (.5 * 16 = 8)
                3082/16 = 192.625 (.625 * 16 = 10 = A)
                192/16 = 12 = C"

Social-Engineering Countermeasures

Being able to identify how to combat social engineering is critical for any certified ethical hacker. There are a number of ways to do this.

Documented and enforced security policies and security-awareness programs are the most critical component in any information-security program. Good policies and procedures aren't effective if they aren't taught and reinforced to employees. The policies need to be communicated to employees to emphasize their importance and then enforced by management. After receiving security-awareness training, employees will be committed to supporting the security policies of the organization.

The corporate security policy should address how and when accounts are set-up and terminated, how often password are changes, who can access what information and how violations or the policy are to be handled. Also, the help desk procedures for the previous tasks as well as identifying employees for example using an employee number or other information to validate a password change. The destruction of paper documents and physical access restrictions are additional areas the security policy should address. Lastly, the policy should address technical areas such as use of modems and virus control.

One of the advantages of a strong security policy is that it removes the responsibility of employees to make judgment calls regarding a hacker's request. If the requested action is prohibited by the policy, the employee has guidelines for denying it.

The most important countermeasure for social engineering is employee education. All employees should be trained on how to keep confidential data safe. Management teams are involved in the creation and implementation of the security policy so that they fully understand it and support it throughout the organization. The company security-awareness policy should require all new employees to go through a security orientation. Annual classes should be required to provide refreshers and updated information for employees.

Another way to increase involvement is through a monthly newsletter with security-awareness articles.

Exam Essentials

Understand the difference between human-based and computer-based social-engineering attacks.   Human-based social engineering uses nontechnical methods to initiate an attack whereas computer-based social engineering employs a computer.

Know the types of human-based social-engineering attacks.   Impersonation, posing as important user, the third-person approach, posing as technical support, shoulder surfing, and dumpster diving are types of human-based social engineering.

Know the types of computer-based social engineering attacks.   E-mail attachments, fake websites, pop-up windows, and reverse social engineering are all computer based social engineering methods.

Understand the importance of employee education.   Educating employees on the signs of social engineering, and the company's security policy is key to preventing social-engineering attacks.

Know the components of social-engineering security policies.   The security policies include policies on how to set up accounts, how often to change passwords, who gets access to what information, how the help desk verifies employee identity, and destruction of paper documents.

Review Questions

1. Which are the four regional Internet registries?

   A. APNIC, PICNIC, NANIC, RIPE NCC

   B. APNIC, MOSTNIC, ARIN, RIPE NCC

   C. APNIC, PICNIC, NANIC, ARIN

   D. APNIC, LACNIC, ARIN, RIPE NCC

2. Which of the following is a tool for performing footprinting undetected?

   A. Whois search

   B. Traceroute

   C. Ping sweep

   D. Host scanning

3. Which of the following tools are used for footprinting? (Choose 3 answers.)

   A. Whois

   B. Sam Spade

   C. NMAP

   D. SuperScan

   E. Nslookup

4. What is the next step to be performed after footprinting?

   A. Scanning

   B. Enumeration

   C. System hacking

   D. Active information gathering

5. Which are good sources of information about a company or its employees? (Choose all that apply.)

   A. Newsgroups

   B. Job postings

   C. Company website

   D. Press releases

6. How does traceroute work?

   A. It uses an ICMP destination-unreachable message to elicit the name of a router.

   B. It sends a specially crafted IP packet to a router to locate the number of hops from the sender to the destination network.

   C. It uses a protocol that will be rejected by the gateway to determine the location.

   D. It uses the TTL value in an ICMP message to determine the number of hops from the sender to the router.

7. What is footprinting?

  A. Measuring the shoe size of an ethical hacker

  B. Accumulation of data by gathering information on a target

  C. Scanning a target network to detect operating system types

  D. Mapping the physical layout of a target's network

8. Nslookup can be used to gather information regarding which of the following?

  A. Host names and IP addresses

  B. Whois information

  C. DNS server locations

  D. Name server types and operating systems

9. Which of the following is a type of social engineering?

  A. Shoulder surfing

  B. User identification

  C. System monitoring

  D. Face-to-face communication

10. Which is an example of social engineering?

  A. A user who holds open the front door of an office for a potential hacker

  B. Calling a help desk and convincing them to reset a password for a user account

  C. Installing a hardware keylogger on a victim's system to capture passwords

  D. Accessing a database with a cracked password

11. What is the best way to prevent a social-engineering attack?

  A. Installing a firewall to prevent port scans

  B. Configuring an IDS to detect intrusion attempts

  C. Increasing the number of help-desk personnel

  D. Employee training and education

12. Which of the following is the best example of reverse social engineering?

  A. A hacker pretends to be a person of authority in order to get a user to give them information.

  B. A help-desk employee pretends to be a person of authority.

  C. A hacker tries to get a user to change their password.

  D. A user changes their password.

13. Using pop-up windows to get a user to give out information is which type of social engineering attack?

  A. Human-based

  B. Computer-based

  C. Nontechnical

  D. Coercive

14. What is it called when a hacker pretends to be a valid user on the system?

  A. Impersonation

  B. Third-person authorization

  C. Help desk

  D. Valid user

15. What is the best reason to implement a security policy?

  A. It increases security.

  B. It makes security harder to enforce.

  C. It removes the employee's responsibility to make judgments.

  D. It decreases security.

16. Faking a website for the purpose of getting a user's password and username is which type of social engineering attack?

  A. Human-based

  B. Computer-based

  C. Web-based

  D. User-based

17. Dumpster diving can be considered which type of social engineering attack?

  A. Human-based

  B. Computer-based

  C. Physical access

  D. Paper-based

Answers to Review Questions

1. D. The four Internet registries are ARIN (American Registry of Internet Numbers), RIPE NCC (Europe, the Middle East, and parts of Central Asia), LACNIC (Latin American and Caribbean Internet Addresses Registry), and APNIC (Asia Pacific Network Information Centre).

2. A. Whois is the only tool listed that won't trigger an IDS alert or otherwise be detected by an organization.

3. A, B, E. Whois, Sam Spade, and nslookup are all used to passively gather information about a target. NMAP and SuperScan are host and network scanning tools.

4. A. According to CEH methodology, scanning occurs after footprinting.

5. A, B, C, D. Newsgroups, job postings, company websites, and press releases are all good sources for information gathering.

6. D. Traceroute uses the TTL values to determine how many hops the router is from the sender. Each router decrements the TTL by one under normal conditions.

7. B. Footprinting is gathering information about a target organization.

8. A. Nslookup queries a DNS server for DNS records such as host names and IP addresses.

9. A. Of the choices listed here, shoulder surfing is considered a type of social engineering.

10. B. Calling a help desk and convincing them to reset a password for a user account is an example of social engineering.

11. D. Employee training and education is the best way to prevent a social-engineering attack.

12. A. When a hacker pretends to be a person of authority in order to get a user to ask them for information, it's an example of reverse social engineering.

13. B. Pop-up windows are a method of getting information from a user utilizing a computer.

14. A. Impersonation involves a hacker pretending to be a valid user on the system.

15. C. Security policies remove the employee's responsibility to make judgments regarding a potential social-engineering attack.

16. B. Website faking is a form of computer-based social engineering attack.

17. A. Dumpster diving is a human-based social engineering attack.

Chapter 3

Scanning and Enumeration

CEH EXAM OBJECTIVES COVERED IN THIS CHAPTER:

✓ **Scanning**

- Define the Terms Port Scanning, Network Scanning, and Vulnerability Scanning
- Understand the CEH Scanning Methodology
- Understand Ping Sweep Techniques
- Understand Nmap Command Switches
- Understand SYN, Stealth, XMAS, NULL, IDLE, and FIN Scans
- List TCP Communication Flag Types
- Understand War Dialing Techniques
- Understand Banner Grabbing and OS Fingerprinting Techniques
- Understand How Proxy Servers Are Used in Launching an Attack
- How Do Anonymizers Work?
- Understand HTTP Tunneling Techniques
- Understand IP Spoofing Techniques

✓ **Enumeration**

- What Is Enumeration?
- What Is Meant by Null Sessions?
- What Is SNMP Enumeration?
- What Are the Steps Involved in Performing Enumeration?

Scanning and enumeration are the first phases of hacking and involve the hacker locating target systems or networks. Enumeration is the follow-on step once scanning is complete and is used to identify computer names, usernames, and shares. Scanning and enumeration are discussed together because many hacking tools perform both.

Scanning

During scanning, the hacker continues to gather information regarding the network and its individual host systems. Data such as IP addresses, operating system, services, and installed applications can help the hacker decide which type of exploit to use in hacking a system. *Scanning* is the process of locating systems that are alive and responding on the network. Ethical hackers use it to identify target systems' IP addresses.

Define the Terms Port Scanning, Network Scanning, and Vulnerability Scanning

After the active and passive reconnaissance stages of system hacking have been completed, scanning is performed. Scanning is used to determine whether a system is on the network and available. Scanning tools are used to gather information about a system such as IP addresses, the operating system, and services running on the target computer.

Table 3.1 lists the three types of scanning.

TABLE 3.1   Types of Scanning

Scanning Type	Purpose
Port scanning	Determines open ports and services
Network scanning	IP addresses
Vulnerability scanning	Presence of known weaknesses

Port scanning   Port scanning is the process of identifying open and available TCP/IP ports on a system. Port-scanning tools enable a hacker to learn about the services available on a given system. Each service or application on a machine is associated with a *well-known* port number. For example, a port-scanning tool that identifies port 80 as open indicates a web server is running on that system. Hackers need to be familiar with well-known port numbers.

On Windows systems, well-known port numbers are located in the C:\windows\system32\drivers\etc\services file. Services file is a hidden file. To view it, show hidden files in Windows Explorer, double-click the file, and open it with Notepad. The CEH exam expects you to know the well-known port numbers for common applications; familiarize yourself with the port numbers for FTP (21), Telnet (23), HTTP (80), SMTP (25), POP3 (110), and HTTPS (443).

Network scanning   Network scanning is a procedure for identifying active hosts on a network, either to attack them or as a network security assessment. Hosts are identified by their individual IP addresses. Network-scanning tools attempt to identify all the *live* or responding hosts on the network and their corresponding IP addresses.

Vulnerability scanning   Vulnerability scanning is the process of proactively identifying the vulnerabilities of computer systems on a network. Generally, a vulnerability scanner first identifies the operating system and version number, including service packs that may be installed. Then, the vulnerability scanner identifies weaknesses or vulnerabilities in the operating system. During the later attack phase, a hacker can exploit those weaknesses in order to gain access to the system.

An intrusion detection system (IDS) or a sophisticated network security professional with the proper tools can detect active port-scanning activity. Scanning tools probe TCP/IP ports looking for open ports and IP addresses, and these probes can be recognized by most security intrusion detection tools. Network and vulnerability scanning can usually be detected as well, because the scanner must interact with the target system over the network.

Understand the CEH Scanning Methodology

As a CEH, you're expected to be familiar with the scanning methodology presented in Figure 3.1. This methodology is the process by which a hacker scans the network. It ensures that no system or vulnerability is overlooked and that the hacker gathers all necessary information to perform an attack.

We'll look at the various stages of this scanning methodology throughout this book, starting with the first three steps—checking for systems that are live and for open ports and service identification the following section.

FIGURE 3.1   CEH scanning methodology

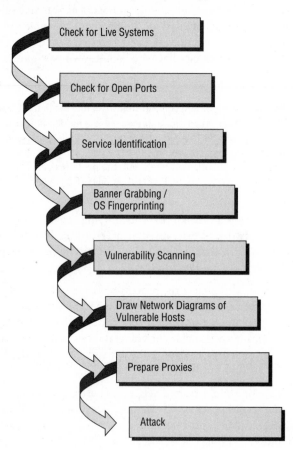

Understand Ping Sweep Techniques

The CEH scanning methodology starts with checking for systems that are live on the network, meaning that they respond to probes or connection requests. The simplest, although not necessarily the most accurate, way to determine whether systems are live is to perform a *ping sweep* of the IP address range. All systems that respond with a ping reply are considered live on the network.

Internet Control Message Protocol (ICMP) scanning is the process of sending an ICMP request or ping to all hosts on the network to determine which ones are up and responding to pings. A benefit of ICMP scanning is that it can be run in *parallel*, meaning all system are scanned at the same time; thus it can run quickly on an entire network. Most hacking tools include a ping-sweep option, which essentially means performing an ICMP request to every host on the network.

One considerable problem with this method is that personal firewall software and network-based firewalls can block a system from responding to ping sweeps. Another problem is that the computer must be on to be scanned.

Hacking Tools

Pinger, Friendly Pinger, and WS_Ping_Pro are all tools that perform ICMP queries. You should be familiar with all these tools for the exam.

Detecting Ping Sweeps

Almost any IDS or intrusion prevention system (IPS) system will detect and alert the security administrator to a ping sweep occurring on the network. Most firewall and proxy servers block ping responses so a hacker can't accurately determine whether systems are available using a ping sweep alone. More intense port scanning must be used if systems don't respond to a ping sweep. Just because a ping sweep doesn't return any active hosts on the network doesn't mean they aren't available—you need to try an alternate method of identification. Remember, hacking takes time, patience, and persistence.

Scanning Ports and Identifying Services

Checking for open ports is the second step in the CEH scanning methodology. *Port scanning* is the method used to check for open ports. The process of port scanning involves probing each port on a host to determine which ports are open. Port scanning generally yields more valuable information than a ping sweep about the host and vulnerabilities on the system.

Service identification is the third step in the CEH scanning methodology; it's usually performed using the same tools as port scanning. By identifying open ports, a hacker can usually also identify the services associated with that port number.

Port-Scan Countermeasures

Countermeasures are processes or tool sets used by security administrators to detect and possibly thwart port scanning of hosts on their network. The following list of countermeasures should be implemented to prevent a hacker from acquiring information during a port scan:

- Proper security architecture, such as implementation of IDS and firewalls, should be followed.

- Ethical hackers use their tool set to test the scanning countermeasures that have been implemented. Once a firewall is in place, a port-scanning tool should be run against hosts on the network to determine whether the firewall correctly detects and stops the port-scanning activity.

- The firewall should be able to detect the probes sent by port-scanning tools. The firewall should carry out *stateful inspections*, which means it examines the data of the packet and not just the TCP header to determine whether the traffic is allowed to pass through the firewall.

- Network IDS should be used to identify the OS-detection method used by some common hackers tools, such as Nmap.

- Only needed ports should be kept open. The rest should be filtered or blocked.

- The staff of the organization using the systems should be given appropriate training on security awareness. They should also know the various security policies they're required to follow.

Understand Nmap Command Switches

Nmap is a free open source tool that quickly and efficiently performs ping sweeps, port scanning, service identification, IP address detection, and operating system detection. Nmap has the benefit of scanning of large number of machines in a single session. It's supported by many operating systems, including Unix, Windows, and Linux.

The state of the port as determined by an Nmap scan can be open, filtered, or unfiltered. *Open* means that the target machine accepts incoming request on that port. *Filtered* means a firewall or network filter is screening the port and preventing Nmap from discovering whether it's open. *Unfiltered* mean the port is determined to be closed, and no firewall or filter is interfering with the Nmap requests.

Nmap support several types of scans. Table 3.2 details some of the common scan methods.

TABLE 3.2   Nmap Scan Types

Nmap Scan Type	Description
TCP connect	The attacker makes a full TCP connection to the target system.
XMAS tree scan	The attacker checks for TCP services by sending XMAS-tree packets, which are named as such because all the "lights" are on meaning the FIN, URG and PSH flags are set (the meaning of the flags will be discussed later in this chapter).
SYN stealth scan	This is also known as *half-open scanning*. The hacker send a SYN packet and receives a SYN-ACK back from the server. It's stealthy because a full TCP connection isn't opened.
Null scan	This is an advanced scan that may be able to pass through firewalls undetected or modified. Null scan has all flags off or not set. It only works on UNIX systems.
Windows scan	This type of scan is similar to the ACK scan and can also detect open ports.
ACK scan	This type of scan is used to map out firewall rules. ACK scan only works on UNIX.

Nmap has numerous command switches to perform different types of scans. The common command switches are listed in Table 3.3.

TABLE 3.3   Common Nmap Commands

Nmap Command	Scan Performed
-sT	TCP connect scan
-sS	SYN scan
-sF	FIN scan
-sX	XMAS tree scan
-sN	Null scan
-sP	Ping scan
-sU	UDP scan
-sO	Protocol scan
-sA	ACK scan
-sW	Windows scan
-sR	RPC scan
-sL	List / DNS scan
-sI	Idle scan
-Po	Don't ping
-PT	TCP ping
-PS	SYN ping
-PI	ICMP ping
-PB	TCP and ICMP ping
-PB	ICMP timestamp
-PM	ICMP netmask

TABLE 3.3   Common Nmap Commands *(continued)*

Nmap Command	Scan Performed
-oN	Normal output
-oX	XML output
-oG	Greppable output
-oA	All output
-T Paranoid	Serial scan; 300 sec between scans
-T Sneaky	Serial scan; 15 sec between scans
-T Polite	Serial scan; .4 sec between scans
-T Normal	Parallel scan
-T Aggressive	Parallel scan, 300 sec timeout, and 1.25 sec/probe
-T Insane	Parallel scan, 75 sec timeout, and .3 sec/probe

To perform an Nmap scan, at the Windows command prompt, type **Nmap *IPaddress*** followed by any command switches used to perform specific type of scans. For example, to scan the host with the IP address 192.168.0.1 using a TCP connect scan type, enter this command:

```
Nmap 192.168.0.1 -sT
```

Make sure you're familiar with the different types of Nmap scans, the syntax to run Nmap, and how to analyze Nmap results.

Understand SYN, Stealth, XMAS, NULL, IDLE, and FIN Scans

As a CEH, you need to be familiar with the following scans:

SYN   A SYN or stealth scan is also called a half-open scan because it doesn't complete the TCP three-way handshake. The TCP/IP three-way handshake will be covered in the next section. A hacker sends a SYN packet to the target; if a SYN/ACK frame is received back, then it's assumed the target would complete the connect and the port is listening. If a RST is received back from the target, then it's assumed the port isn't active or is closed. The advantage of the SYN stealth scan is that fewer IDS systems log this as an attack or connection attempt.

XMAS   XMAS scans send a packet with the FIN, URG, and PSH flags set. If the port is open, there is no response; but if the post is closed, the target responds with a RST/ACK packet. XMAS scans work only on target systems that follow the RFC 793 implementation of TCP/IP and don't work against any version of Windows.

FIN   A FIN scan is similar to an XMAS scan but sends a packet with just the FIN flag set. FIN scans receive the same response and have the same limitations as XMAS scans.

NULL   A NULL scan is also similar to XMAS and FIN in its limitations and response, but it just sends a packet with no flags set.

IDLE   An IDLE scan uses a spoofed IP address to send a SYN packet to a target. Depending on the response, the port can be determined to be open or closed. IDLE scans determine port scan response by monitoring IP header sequence numbers.

List TCP Communication Flag Types

TCP scan types are built on the *TCP three-way handshake*. TCP connections require a three-way handshake before a connection can be made and data transferred between the sender and receiver. Figure 3.2 details the steps of the TCP three-way handshake.

FIGURE 3.2   TCP three-way handshake

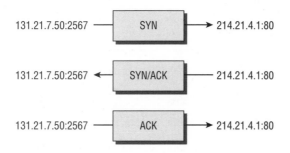

In order to complete the three-way handshake and make a successful connection between two hosts, the sender must send a TCP packet with the synchronize (SYN) bit set. Then, the receiving system responds with a TCP packet with the synchronize (SYN) and acknowledge (ACK) bit set to indicate the host is ready to receive data. The source system sends a final packet with the acknowledge (ACK) bit set to indicate the connection is complete and data is ready to be sent.

Because TCP is a connection-oriented protocol, a process for establishing a connection (three-way handshake), restarting a failed connection, and finishing a connection is part of the protocol. These protocol notifications are called *flags*. TCP contains ACK, RST, SYN, URG, PSH, and FIN flags. The following list identifies the function of the TCP flags:

- SYN—Synchronize. Initiates a connection between hosts.
- ACK—Acknowledge. Established connection between hosts.
- PSH—Push. System is forwarding buffered data.
- URG—Urgent. Data in packets must be processed quickly.
- FIN—Finish. No more transmissions.
- RST—Reset. Resets the connection.

A hacker can attempt to bypass detection by using flags instead of completing a normal TCP connection. The TCP scan types in Table 3.4 are used by some scanning tools to elicit a response from a system by setting one or more flags.

TABLE 3.4   TCP Scan Types

XMAS Scan	Flags sent by hacker
XMAS scan	All flags set (ACK, RST, SYN, URG, PSH, FIN)
FIN scan	FIN
NULL Scan	No flags set
TCP connect / full-open scan	SYN, then ACK
SYN scan / half-open scan	SYN, then RST

Hacking Tools

IPEye is a TCP port scanner that can do SYN, FIN, Null, and XMAS scans. It's a command-line tool.

IPEye probes the ports on a target system and responds with either closed, reject, drop, or open. Closed means there is a computer on the other end, but it doesn't listen at the port. Reject means a firewall is rejecting (sending a reset back) the connection to the port. Drop means a firewall is dropping everything to the port, or there is no computer on the other end. Open means some kind of service is listening at the port. These responses help a hacker identify what type of system is responding.

IPSecScan is a tool that can scan either a single IP address or a range of addresses looking for systems that are IPSec enabled.

Netscan Tools Pro 2000, Hping2, KingPingicmpenum, and SNMP Scanner are all scanning tools and can also be used to fingerprint the operating system (discussed later).

Icmpenum uses not only ICMP Echo packets to probe networks, but also ICMP Timestamp and ICMP Information packets. Furthermore, it supports spoofing and sniffing for reply packets. Icmpenum is great for scanning networks when the firewall blocks ICMP Echo packets but fails to block Timestamp or Information packets.

Hping2 is notable because it contains a host of other features besides OS fingerprinting such as TCP, User Datagram Protocol (UDP), ICMP, and raw-IP ping protocols, traceroute mode, and the ability to send files between the source and target system.

SNMP Scanner allows you to scan a range or list of hosts performing ping, DNS, and Simple Network Management Protocol (SNMP) queries.

Understand War-Dialing Techniques

War dialing is the process of dialing modem numbers to find an open modem connection that provides remote access to a network for an attack to be launched against the target system. The term *war dialing* originates from the early days of the Internet when most companies were connected to the Internet via dial-up modem connections. War dialing is included as a scanning method because it finds another network connection that may have weaker security than the main Internet connection. Many organizations set up remote-access modems that are now antiquated but have failed to remove those remote-access servers. This gives hackers an easy way into the network with much weaker security mechanisms. For example, many remote-access systems use the Password Authentication Protocol (PAP), which send passwords in cleartext, rather than newer VPN technology that encrypts passwords.

War-dialing tools work on the premise that companies don't control the dial-in ports as strictly as the firewall, and machines with modems attached are present everywhere even if those modems are no longer in use. Many servers still have modems with phone lines connected as a backup in case the primary Internet connection fails. These available modem connections can be used by a war-dialing program to gain remote access to the system and internal network.

Hacking Tools

THC-Scan, Phonesweep, war dialer, and telesweep are all tools that identify phone numbers and can dial a target to make a connection with a computer modem. These tools generally work by using a predetermined list of common usernames and passwords in an attempt to gain access to the system. Most remote-access dial-in connections aren't secured with a password or use very rudimentary security.

Understand Banner Grabbing and OS Fingerprinting Techniques

Banner grabbing and operating system identification—which can also be defined as *fingerprinting* the TCP/IP stack—is the fourth step in the CEH scanning methodology. The process of fingerprinting allows the hacker to identify particularly vulnerable or high value targets on the network. Hackers are looking for the easiest way to gain access to a system or network. Banner grabbing is the process of opening a connection and reading the banner or response sent by the application. Many e-mail, FTP, and web servers will respond to a telnet connection with the name and version of the software. The aids a hacker in fingerprinting the OS and application software. For example, a Microsoft Exchange e-mail server would only be installed on Windows OS.

Active stack fingerprinting is the most common form of fingerprinting. It involves sending data to a system to see how the system responds. It's based on the fact that various operating system vendors implement the TCP stack differently, and responses will differ based on the operating system. The responses are then compared to a database to determine the operating system. Active stack fingerprinting is detectable because it repeatedly attempts to connect with the same target system.

Passive stack fingerprinting is stealthier and involves examining traffic on the network to determine the operating system. It uses sniffing techniques instead of scanning techniques. Passive stack fingerprinting usually goes undetected by an IDS or other security system but is less accurate than active fingerprinting.

Drawing Network Diagrams of Vulnerable Hosts

Although it isn't a CEH exam objective, understanding the tools used in step 6 of the CEH scanning methodology—drawing a network diagram of vulnerable hosts—is a must. A number of network-management tools can assist you with this step. Such tools are generally used to manage network devices but can be turned against security administrators by enterprising hackers.

SolarWinds Toolset, Queso, Harris Stat, and Cheops are all network-management tools that can be used for operating system detection, network diagram mapping, listing services running on a network, generalized port scanning, and so on.

These tools diagram entire networks in a GUI interface including routers, servers, hosts and firewalls. Most of these tools can discover IP addresses, host names, services, operating systems, and version information.

Netcraft and HTTrack are tools that fingerprint an operating system. Both are used to determine the OS and web-server software version numbers.

Netcraft is a website that periodically polls web servers to determine the operating system version and the web-server software version. Netcraft can provide useful information the hacker can use in identifying vulnerabilities in the web server software. In addition, Netcraft has an anti-phishing toolbar and web-server verification tool you can use to make sure you're using the actual web server rather than a spoofed web server.

HTTrack arranges the original site's relative link structure. You open a page of the mirrored website in your browser, and then you can browse the site from link to link as if you were viewing it online. HTTrack can also update an existing mirrored site and resume interrupted downloads.

Understand How Proxy Servers Are Used in Launching an Attack

Preparing proxy servers is the last step in the CEH scanning methodology. A *proxy server* is a computer that acts as an intermediary between the hacker and the target computer.

Using a proxy server can allow a hacker to become anonymous on the network. The hacker first makes a connection to the proxy server and then requests a connection to the target computer via the existing connection to the proxy. Essentially, the proxy requests access to the target computer not the hacker's computer. This lets a hacker surf the web anonymously or otherwise hide their attack.

Hacking Tools

SocksChain is a tool that gives a hacker the ability to attack through a chain of proxy servers. The main purpose of doing this is to hide the hacker's real IP address and therefore minimize the chance of detection. When a hacker works through several proxy servers in series, it's much harder to locate the hacker. Tracking the attacker's IP address through the logs of several proxy servers is complex and tedious work. If one of the proxy servers' log files is lost or incomplete, the chain is broken, and the hacker's IP address remains anonymous.

How Do Anonymizers Work?

Anonymizers are services that attempt to make web surfing anonymous by utilizing a website that acts as a proxy server for the web client. The first anonymizer software tool was developed by Anonymizer.com; it was created in 1997 by Lance Cottrell. The anonymizer removes all the identifying information from a user's computers while the user surfs the Internet, thereby ensuring the privacy of the user.

To visit a website anonymously, the hacker enters the website address into the anonymizer software, and the anonymizer software makes the request to the selected site. All requests and web pages are relayed through the anonymizer site, making it difficult to track the actual requester of the webpage.

Understand HTTP Tunneling Techniques

A popular method of bypassing a firewall or IDS is to tunnel a blocked protocol (such as SMTP) through an allowed protocol (such as HTTP). Almost all IDS and firewalls act as a proxy between a client's PC and the Internet and pass only the traffic defined as being allowed.

Most companies allow HTTP traffic because it's usually benign web access. However, a hacker using a HTTP tunneling tool can subvert the proxy by hiding potentially destructive protocols, such as IM or chat, within an innocent-looking protocol packet.

Hacking Tools

HTTPort, Tunneld, and BackStealth are all tools to tunnel traffic though HTTP. They allow the bypassing of an HTTP proxy, which blocks certain protocols access to the Internet. These tools allow the following potentially dangerous software protocols to be used from behind an HTTP proxy:

- E-mail

- IRC

- ICQ

- News

- AIM

- FTP

Understand IP Spoofing Techniques

A hacker can *spoof* an IP address when scanning target systems to minimize the chance of detection. One drawback of spoofing an IP address is that a TCP session can't be successfully completed.

Source routing lets an attacker specify the route that a packet takes through the Internet. This can also minimize the chance of detection by bypassing IDS and firewalls that may block or detect the attack. Source routing uses a reply address in the IP header to return the packet to a spoofed address instead of the attacker's real address.

To detect IP address spoofing, you can compare the time to live (TTL) values: The attacker's TTL will be different from the spoofed address's real TTL.

Exam Essentials

Know the three type of scanning.   Port, network, and vulnerability scanning are the three types of scanning.

Know how to determine which systems are alive on the network.   Know how to use ICMP query tools to perform ping sweeps to determine which systems are responding. Ping sweeps have limitations, and some systems may not respond to the ICMP queries.

Know how to perform port scanning using nmap.   Learn the switches for performing nmap scanning using the nmap command. For example: `nmap -sS` performs a SYN scan.

Understand the uses and limitations of different scan types.   Make sure you're familiar with TCP connect, SYN, NULL, IDLE, FIN, and XMAS scans and when each type should be used.

Understand the process of the TCP three-way handshake.   The TCP connection process starts with a SYN packet sent to the target system. The target system responds with a SYN+ACK packet, and the source system sends back an ACK packet to the target. This completes a successful TCP connection.

Be familiar with port-scanning countermeasures.   Implement firewalls that prevent internal systems from being scanned by blocking ping sweeps and port-scanning tools such as nmap. IDSs and IPSs can alert an administrator to a scan taking place on the network.

Know the uses of war dialing.   War dialing is used to test dial-in remote access system security. Phone numbers are dialed randomly in an attempt to make an unsecured modem connection and gain access to the network.

Understand how to perform operating system fingerprinting using active and passive methods.   Active fingerprinting means sending a request to a system to see how it responds (banner grabbing, for example). Passive fingerprinting is examining traffic sent to and from the system to determine the operating system.

Know how to surf the web anonymously using an anonymizer.   Use a website anonymizer to hide the source address to make the system surfing the web appear anonymous.

Understand HTTP tunneling and IP spoofing.   HTTP tunneling and IP spoofing are two methods of hiding the physical address or protocols that a hacker may be using. They're useful in evading firewalls and obfuscating the hacker's identity or whereabouts.

Enumeration

Enumeration occurs after scanning and is the process of gathering and compiling usernames, machine names, network resources, shares, and services. It also refers to actively querying or connecting to a target system to acquire this information.

What Is Enumeration?

The objective of enumeration is to identify a user account or system account for potential use in hacking the target system. It isn't necessary to find a system administrator account, because most account privileges can be escalated to allow the account more access than was previously granted.

 The process of privilege escalation is covered in the next chapter.

Many hacking tools are designed for scanning IP networks to locate NetBIOS name information. For each responding host, the tools list IP address, NetBIOS computer name, logged-in username, and MAC address information.

On a Windows 2000 domain, the built-in tool `net view` can be used for NetBIOS enumeration. To enumerate NetBIOS names using the `net view` command, enter the following at the command prompt:

```
net view / domain
nbtstat -A IP address
```

Hacking Tools

DumpSec is a NetBIOS enumeration tool. It connects to the target system as a null user with the `net use` command. It then enumerates users, groups, NTFS permissions, and file ownership information.

Hyena is a tool that enumerates NetBIOS shares and additionally can exploit the null session vulnerability to connect to the target system and change the share path or edit the registry.

The SMB Auditing Tool is a password-auditing tool for the Windows and Server Message Block (SMB) platforms. Windows uses SMB to communicate between the client and server. The SMB Auditing Tool is able to identify usernames and crack passwords on Windows systems.

The NetBIOS Auditing Tool is another NetBIOS enumeration tool. It's used to perform various security checks on remote servers running NetBIOS file sharing services.

What Is Meant by Null Sessions?

A null session occurs when you log in to a system with no username or password. NetBIOS null sessions are a vulnerability found in the Common Internet File System (CIFS) or SMB, depending on the operating system.

Microsoft Windows uses SMB, and Unix/Linux systems use CIFS.

Once a hacker has made a NetBIOS connection using a null session to a system, they can easily get a full dump of all usernames, groups, shares, permissions, policies, services and more using the Null user account. The SMB and NetBIOS standards in Windows include APIs that return information about a system via TCP port 139.

One method of connecting a NetBIOS null session to a Windows system is to use the hidden Inter Process Communication share (IPC$). This hidden share is accessible using the `net use` command. As mentioned earlier, the `net use` command is a built-in Windows command that connects to a share on another computer. The empty quotation marks (`""`) indicate that you want to connect with no username and no password. To make a NetBIOS null session to a system with the IP address 192.21.7.1 with the built-in anonymous user account and a null password using the `net use` command, the syntax is as follows:

```
C: \> net use \\192.21.7.1 \IPC$ " " /u: " "
```

Once the `net use` command has been successfully completed, the hacker has a channel over which to use other hacking tools and techniques.

As a CEH, you need to know how to defend against NetBIOS enumeration and null sessions. We'll discuss that in the following section.

NetBIOS Enumeration and Null Session Countermeasures

The NetBIOS null session use specific port numbers on the target machine. Null sessions require access to TCP ports 135, 137,139, and/or 445. One countermeasure is to close these ports on the target system. This can be accomplished by disabling SMB services on individual hosts by unbinding the TCP/IP WINS client from the interface in the network connection's properties. To implement this countermeasure, perform the following steps:

1. Open the properties of the network connection.

2. Click TCP/IP and then the Properties button.

3. Click the Advanced button.

4. On the WINS tab, select disable NetBIOS Over TCP/IP.

A security administrator can also edit the registry directly to restrict the anonymous user from login. To implement this countermeasure, perform the following steps:

1. Open regedt32, and navigate to `HKLM\SYSTEM\CurrentControlSet\LSA`.

2. Choose Edit ➢ Add Value. Enter these values:

   - Value name: **RestrictAnonymous**

   - Data Type: **REG_WORD**

   - Value: **2**

Finally, the system can be upgraded to Windows XP and the latest Microsoft security patches, which mitigates the NetBIOS null session vulnerability from occurring.

What Is SNMP Enumeration?

SNMP enumeration is the process of using SNMP to enumerate user accounts on a target system. SNMP employs two major types of software components for communication: the SNMP agent, which is located on the networking device; and the SNMP management station, which communicates with the agent.

Almost all network infrastructure devices, such as routers and switches and including Windows systems, contain an SNMP agent to manage the system or device. The SNMP management station sends requests to agents, and the agents send back replies. The requests and replies refer to configuration variables accessible by agent software. Management stations can also send requests to set values for certain variables. Traps let the management station know that something significant has happened in the agent software such as a reboot or an interface failure. Management Information Base (MIB) is the database of configuration variables, which resides on the networking device.

SNMP has two passwords you can use to access and configure the SNMP agent from the management station. The first is called a *read community string*. This password lets you view the configuration of the device or system. The second is called the *read/write community string*; it's for changing or editing the configuration on the device. Generally, the default read community string is public and the default read/write community string is private. A common security loophole occurs when the community strings are left at the default settings: A hacker can use these default passwords to view or change the device configuration.

 If you have any questions about how easy it is to locate the default passwords of devices, look at the website www.defaultpassword.com.

Hacking Tools

SNMPUtil and IP Network Browser are SNMP enumeration tools.

SNMPUtil gathers Windows user account information via SNMP in Windows systems. Some information such as routing tables, ARP tables, IP addresses, MAC addresses, TCP and UDP open ports, user accounts, and shares can be read from a Windows system that has SNMP enabled using the SNMPUtil tools.

IP Network Browser from the SolarWinds toolset also uses SNMP to gather more information about a device that has an SNMP agent.

SNMP Enumeration Countermeasures

The simplest way to prevent SNMP enumeration is to remove the SNMP agent on the potential target systems or turn off the SNMP service. If shutting off SNMP isn't an option, then change the default read and read/write community names.

In addition, an administrator can implement the Group Policy security option Additional Restrictions For Anonymous Connections, which restricts SNMP connections.

Group Policy is implemented on a Windows domain controller. Network administrators should be familiar with how to do this. It's outside the scope of this book, because many steps are involved in performing this task.

Windows 2000 DNS Zone Transfer

In a Windows 2000 domain, clients use service (SRV) records to locate Windows 2000 domain services, such as Active Directory and Kerberos. This means every Windows 2000 Active Directory domain must have a DNS server for the network to operate properly.

A simple zone transfer performed with the `nslookup` command can enumerate lots of interesting network information. The command to enumerate using the `nslookup` command is as follows:

```
nslookup ls -d domainname
```

Within the `nslookup` results, a hacker looks closely at the following records, because they provide additional information about the network services:

- Global Catalog service (`_gc._tcp_`)
- Domain controllers (`_ldap._tcp`)
- Kerberos authentication (`_kerberos._tcp`)

As a countermeasure, zone transfers can be blocked in the properties of the Windows DNS server.

An Active Directory database is a Lightweight Directory Access Protocol (LDAP) based database. This allows the existing users and groups in the database to be enumerated with a simple LDAP query. The only thing required to perform this enumeration is to create an authenticated session via LDAP. A Windows 2000 LDAP client called the Active Directory Administration Tool (`ldp.exe`) connects to an Active Directory server and identifies the contents of the database. You can find `ldp.exe` on the Windows 2000 CD-ROM in the `Support\Reskit\Netmgmt\Dstool` folder.

To perform an Active Directory enumeration attack, a hacker performs the following steps:

1. Connect to any Active Directory server using `ldp.exe` on port 389. When the connection is complete, server information is displayed in the right pane.

2. On the Connection Menu, choose to authenticate. Type the username, password, and domain name in the appropriate boxes. You can use the Guest account or any other domain account.

3. Once the authentication is successful, enumerate users and built-in groups by choosing the Search option from the Browse menu.

Hacking Tools

User2SID and SID2User are command-line tools that look up Windows service identifiers (SIDs from username input and vice versa.)

Enum is a command-line enumeration utility. It uses null sessions and can retrieve usernames, machine names, shares, group and membership lists, passwords, and Local Security policy information. Enum is also capable of brute-force dictionary attacks on individual accounts.

UserInfo is a command-line tools that's used to gather usernames and that can also be used to create new user accounts.

GetAcct is a GUI-based tool that enumerates user accounts on a system.

SMBBF is a SMB brute-force tool that tries to determine user accounts and accounts with blank passwords.

What Are the Steps Involved in Performing Enumeration?

Hackers need to be methodical in their approach to hacking. The following steps are an example of those a hacker might perform in preparation for hacking a target system:

1. Extract usernames using enumeration.
2. Gather information about the host using null sessions.
3. Perform Windows enumeration using the Superscan tool.
4. Acquire the user accounts using the tool GetAcct.
5. Perform SNMP port scanning.

Exam Essentials

Understand how to enumerate user accounts.   Enumeration involves making active connections to systems through either SMB/CIFS or NetBIOS vulnerabilities and querying the system for information.

Be aware of the type of information that can be enumerated on a system.   The type of information enumerated by hackers includes network resources and shares, users and groups, and applications and banners.

Understand null sessions.   Connecting to a system using a blank password is known as a Null Session. Null sessions are often used by hackers to connect to target systems and then run enumeration tools against the system.

Know the types of enumeration tools.   NetBIOS and SNMP enumerations can be performed using tools such as SNMPUtil, and Enum.

Know how to perform a DNS zone transfer on Windows 2000 computers.   Nslookup can be used to perform a DNS zone transfer.

Understand null session enumeration countermeasures.   Use a firewall to block ports 135 and 139, or patch the registry to prevent null sessions.

Understand SNMP enumeration countermeasures.   Turn off the SNMP services, or change the default read and read/write community names.

Know how to identify vulnerable accounts.   Tools such as User2SID, SID2User, and UserInfo can be used to identify vulnerable user accounts.

Review Questions

1. What port number does FTP use?
   A. 21
   B. 25
   C. 23
   D. 80

2. What port number does HTTPS use?
   A. 443
   B. 80
   C. 53
   D. 21

3. What is war dialing used for?
   A. Testing firewall security
   B. Testing remote access system security
   C. Configuring a proxy filtering gateway
   D. Configuring a firewall

4. Banner grabbing is an example of what?
   A. Passive operating system fingerprinting
   B. Active operating system fingerprinting
   C. Footprinting
   D. Application analysis

5. What are the three types of scanning?
   A. Port, network, and vulnerability
   B. Port, network, and services
   C. Grey, black, and white hat
   D. Server, client, and network

6. What is the main problem with using only ICMP queries for scanning?
   A. The port is not always available.
   B. The protocol is unreliable.
   C. Systems may not respond because of a firewall.
   D. Systems may not have the service running.

7. What does the TCP RST command do?

   A. Starts a TCP connection

   B. Restores the connection to a previous state

   C. Finishes a TCP connections

   D. Resets the TCP connection

8. What is the proper sequence of a TCP connection?

   A. SYN-SYN ACK-ACK

   B. SYN-ACK-FIN

   C. SYN-SYNACK-ACK

   D. SYN-PSH-ACK

9. A packet with all flags set is which type of scan?

   A. Full Open

   B. Syn scan

   C. XMAS

   D. TCP connect

10. What is the proper command to perform and NMAP SYN scan every 5 minutes?

   A. `nmap -ss - paranoid`

   B. `nmap -Ss -paranoid`

   C. `nmap -Ss -fast`

   D. `namp -Ss -sneaky`

11. In order to prevent a hacker from using SMB session hijacking, which TCP and UDP ports would you block at the firewall?

   A. 167 and 137

   B. 80 and 23

   C. 139 and 445

   D. 1277 and 1270

12. Why would an attacker want to perform a scan on port 137?

   A. To locate the FTP service on the target host

   B. To check for file and print sharing on Windows systems

   C. To discover proxy servers on a network

   D. To discover a target system with the NetBIOS null session vulnerability

13. SNMP is a protocol used to manage network infrastructure devices. What is the SNMP read/write community name used for?

    A. Viewing the configuration information

    B. Changing the configuration information

    C. Monitoring the device for errors

    D. Controlling the SNMP management station

14. Why would the network security team be concerned about ports 135–139 being open on a system?

    A. SMB is enabled, and the system is susceptible to null sessions.

    B. SMB is not enabled, and the system is susceptible to null sessions.

    C. Windows RPC is enabled, and the system is susceptible to Windows DCOM remote sessions.

    D. Windows RPC is not enabled, and the system is susceptible to Windows DCOM remote sessions.

15. Which step comes after enumerating users in the CEH hacking cycle?

    A. Crack password

    B. Escalate privileges

    C. Scanning

    D. Covering tracks

16. What is enumeration?

    A. Identifying active systems on the network

    B. Cracking passwords

    C. Identifying users and machine names

    D. Identifying routers and firewalls

17. What is a command-line tool used to look up a username from a SID?

    A. UsertoSID

    B. Userenum

    C. SID2User

    D. Getacct

18. Which tool can be used to perform a DNS zone transfer on Windows?

    A. `nslookup`

    B. `DNSlookup`

    C. `whois`

    D. `ipconfig`

19. What is a null session?

    A. Connecting to a system with the administrator username and password

    B. Connecting to a system with the admin username and password

    C. Connecting to a system with a random username and password

    D. Connecting to a system with no username and password

20. What is a countermeasure for SNMP enumeration?

    A. Remove the SNMP agent from the device.

    B. Shut down ports 135 and 139 at the firewall.

    C. Shut down ports 80 and 443 at the firewall.

    D. Enable SNMP read-only security on the agent device.

Answers to Review Questions

1. A. FTP uses TCP port 21. This is a well-known port number and can be found in the Windows `services` file.

2. A. HTTPS uses TCP port 443. This is a well-known port number and can be found in the Windows `services` file.

3. B. War dialing involves placing calls to a series of numbers in hopes that a modem will answer the call. It can be used to test the security of a remote-access system.

4. A. Banner grabbing is not detectible; therefore it is considered passive OS fingerprinting.

5. A. Port, network, and vulnerability are the three types of scanning.

6. C. Systems may not respond to ICMP because they have firewall software installed that blocks the responses.

7. D. The TCP RST command resets the TCP connection.

8. A. A SYN packet is followed by a SYN-ACK packet. Then, an ACK finishes a successful TCP connection.

9. C. An XMAS scan has all flags set.

10. B. The command `nmap -Ss - paranoid` performs a SYN scan every 300 seconds or 5 minutes.

11. C. Block the ports used by NetBIOS null sessions. These are 139 and 445.

12. D. Port 137 is used for NetBIOS null sessions.

13. B. The SNMP read/write community name is the password used to make changes to the device configuration.

14. A. Ports in the 135 to 139 range indicate the system has SMB services running and is susceptible to null sessions.

15. A. Password cracking is the next step in the CEH hacking cycle after enumerating users.

16. C. Enumeration is the process of finding usernames, machine names, network shares, and services on the network.

17. C. SID2User is a command-line tool to find a username from a SID.

18. A. `nslookup` is a Windows tool that can be used to initiate a DNS zone transfer that sends all the DNS records to a hacker's system.

19. D. A null session involves connecting to a system with no username and password.

20. A. The best countermeasure to SNMP enumeration is to remove the SNMP agent from the device. Doing so prevents it from responding to SNMP requests.

Chapter

4

System Hacking

CEH EXAM OBJECTIVES COVERED IN THIS CHAPTER:

- ✓ Understanding Password-Cracking Techniques
- ✓ Understanding Different Types of Passwords
- ✓ Understand Escalating privileges
- ✓ Understanding Keyloggers and Other Spyware Technologies
- ✓ Understanding Rootkits
- ✓ Understanding How to Hide Files
- ✓ Understanding Steganography Technologies
- ✓ Understanding How to Cover Your Tracks and Erase Evidences

In this chapter, we'll look at the various aspects of system hacking. As you recall from Chapter 3, "Scanning and Enumeration," the system hacking cycle consists of six steps. The first step—enumeration—was discussed in the previous chapter. This chapter covers the five remaining steps:

- Cracking passwords
- Escalating privileges
- Executing applications
- Hiding files
- Covering tracks

Understanding Password-Cracking Techniques

Many hacking attempts start with attempting to crack passwords. Passwords are the key piece of information needed to access a system. Users, when creating passwords, often select passwords that are prone to being cracked. Many reuse passwords or choose one that's simple—such as a pet's name—to help them remember it. Because of this human factor, most password cracking is successful; it can be the launching point for escalating privileges, executing applications, hiding files, and covering tracks. Passwords may be cracked manually or with automated tools such as a dictionary or brute-force method, each of which are covered later in this chapter.

Manual password cracking involves attempting to log on with different passwords. The hacker follows these steps:

1. Find a valid user account (such as Administrator or Guest).
2. Create a list of possible passwords.
3. Rank the passwords from high to low probability.
4. Key in each password.
5. Try again until a successful password is found.

A hacker can also create a script file that tries each password in a list. This is still considered manual cracking, but it's time consuming and not usually effective.

A more efficient way of cracking a password is to gain access to the password file on a system. Most systems *hash* (one-way encrypt) a password for storage on a system. During the logon process, the password entered by the user is hashed using the same algorithm and then compared to the hashed passwords stored in the file. A hacker can attempt to gain access to the hashing algorithm stored on the server instead of trying to guess or otherwise identify the password. If the hacker is successful, they can decrypt the passwords stored on the server.

 Passwords are stored in the Security Accounts Manager (SAM) file on a Windows system and in a password shadow file on a Linux system.

Hacking Tools

Legion automates the password guessing in NetBIOS sessions. Legion scans multiple IP address ranges for Windows shares and also offers a manual dictionary attack tool.

NTInfoScan is a security scanner for NT 4.0. This vulnerability scanner produces an HTML-based report of security issues found on the target system and other information.

L0phtCrack is a password auditing and recovery package distributed by @stake software, which is now owned by Symantec. It performs Server Message Block (SMB) packet captures on the local network segment and captures individual login sessions. L0phtCrack contains dictionary, brute-force, and hybrid attack capabilities.

John the Ripper is a command-line tool designed to crack both Unix and NT passwords. The cracked passwords are case insensitive and may not represent the real mixed-case password.

KerbCrack consists of two programs: kerbsniff and kerbcrack. The sniffer listens on the network and captures Windows 2000/XP Kerberos logins. The cracker can be used to find the passwords from the capture file using a brute force attack or a dictionary attack.

Understanding the LanManager Hash

Windows 2000 uses NT Lan Manager (NTLM) hashing to secure passwords in transit on the network. Depending on the password, NTLM hashing can be weak and easy to break. For example, let's say that the password is 123456abcdef. When this password is encrypted with the NTLM algorithm, it's first converted to all uppercase: 123456ABCDEF. The password is padded with null (blank) characters to make it 14 characters long: 123456ABCDEF__. Before the password is encrypted, the 14-character string is split in half: 123456A and BCDEF__. Each string is individually encrypted, and the results are concatenated:

```
123456A = 6BF11E04AFAB197F
BCDEF__ = F1E9FFDCC75575B15
```

The hash is 6BF11E04AFAB197FF1E9FFDCC75575B15

The first half of the password contains alphanumeric characters; L0phtCrack will take 24 hours to crack this part. The second half contains only letters and symbols and will take 60 seconds to crack. This is because there are many fewer combinations in the second half of the hashed password. If the password is seven characters or fewer the second half of the hash will always be AAD3B435B51404EE.

Cracking Windows 2000 Passwords

The SAM file in Windows contains the usernames and hashed passwords. It's located in the Windows\system32\config directory. The file is locked when the operating system is running so a hacker can't attempt to copy the file while the machine is booted to Windows.

One option for copying the SAM file is to boot to an alternate operating system such as DOS or Linux with a boot CD. Alternately, the file can be copied from the repair directory. If a systems administrator uses the RDISK feature of Windows to back up the system, then a compressed copy of the SAM file called SAM._ is created in C:\windows\repair. To expand this file, use the following command at the command prompt:

```
C:\>expand sam._ sam
```

After the file is uncompressed, a dictionary, hybrid, or brute-force attack can be run against the SAM file using a tool like L0phtCrack.

Hacking Tools

Win32CreateLocalAdminUser is a program that creates a new user with the username and password X and adds the user to the local administrator's group. This action is part of the Metasploit Project and can be launched with the Metasploit framework on Windows.

Offline NT Password Resetter is a method of resetting the password to the administrator's account when the system isn't booted to Windows. The most common method is to boot to a Linux boot CD and then access the NTFS partition, which is no longer protected, and change the password.

Redirecting the SMB Logon to the Attacker

Another way to discover passwords on a network is to redirect the Server Message Block (SMB) logon to an attacker's computer so that the passwords are sent to the hacker. In order to do this, the hacker must sniff the NTLM responses from the authentication server and trick the victim into attempting Windows authentication with the attacker's computer. A common technique is to send the victim an e-mail message with an embedded hyperlink to a fraudulent

process and can then be compared against a dictionary file or word list. User account passwords are commonly *hashed* or encrypted when sent on the network to prevent unauthorized access and use. If the password is protected by encryption or hashing, then special tools in the hacker's toolkit can be used to break the algorithm.

Cracking the password-hashing will be discussed later in this chapter.

Another passive online attack is known as *man-in-the-middle* (MITM). In a MITM attack, the hacker intercepts the authentication request and forwards it to the server. By inserting a sniffer between the client and the server, the hacker is able to sniff both connections and capture passwords in the process.

A *replay attack* is also a passive online attack; it occurs when the hacker intercepts the password en route to the authentication server and then captures and resends the authentication packets for later authentication. In this manner, the hacker doesn't have to break the password or learn the password through MITM but rather captures the password and reuses the password-authentication packets later to authenticate as the client.

Active Online Attacks

The easiest way to gain Administrator-level access to a system is to guess a simple password assuming the administrator used a simple password. Password guessing is an active online attack. It relies on the human factor involved in password creation and only works on weak passwords.

In Chapter 3, when we discussed the Enumeration phase of system hacking, you learned the vulnerability of NetBIOS enumeration and null sessions. Assuming that the NetBIOS TCP 139 port is open, the most effective method of breaking into a Windows NT or Windows 2000 system is password guessing. This is done by attempting to connect to an enumerated share (IPC$ or C$) and trying a username and password combination. The most commonly used Administrator account and password combinations are words like Admin, Administrator, Sysadmin, or Password, or a null password.

A hacker may first try to connect to a default Admin$, C$, or C:\Windows share. To connect to the hidden C: drive share, for example, type the following command in the Run field (Start ➤ Run):

```
\\ip_address\c$
```

Automated programs can quickly generate dictionary files, word lists, or every possible combination of letters, numbers, and special characters and then attempt to log on using those credentials. Most systems prevent this type of attack by setting a maximum number of login attempts on a system before the account is locked.

In the following sections, we'll discuss how hackers can perform automated password guessing more closely, as well as countermeasures to such attacks.

Performing Automated Password Guessing

To speed up the guessing of a password, hackers us automated tools. An easy process for automating password guessing is to use the Windows shell commands based on the standard NET USE syntax. To create a simple automated password-guessing script, perform the following steps:

1. Create a simple username and password file using Windows Notepad. Automated tools such as the Dictionary Generator are available to create this word list. Save the file on the C: drive as `credentials.txt`.

2. Pipe this file using the FOR command:

   `C:\> FOR /F "token=1, 2*" %i in (credentials.txt)`

3. Type **net use \\targetIP\IPC$ %i /u: %j** to use the `credentials.txt` file to attempt to log on to the target system's hidden share.

> Another example of how the FOR command can be used by an attacker is to wipe the contents of the hard with zeros using the command syntax ((i=0; i<11; i++)); do dd if=/dev/random of=/dev/hda && dd if=/dev/zero of=dev/hda done. The wipe command could also be used to perform the wiping of data from the hard disk using the command $ wipe -fik /dev/hda1

Defending Against Password Guessing

Two options exist to defend against password guessing and password attacks. Both smart cards and biometrics add a layer of security to the insecurity that's inherent when users create their own passwords.

A user can also be authenticated and validated using *biometrics*. Biometrics use physical characteristics such as fingerprints, hand geometry scans, and retinal scans as credentials to validate users.

Both smart cards and biometrics use *two-factor authentication*, which requires two forms of identification (such as the actual smart card and a password) when validating a user. By requiring something the user physically has (a smart card, in this instance) and something the user knows (their password), security is increased, and the authentication process isn't susceptible to password attacks.

> RSA Secure ID is a two-factor authentication system that utilized a token and password.

Offline Attacks

Offline attacks are performed from a location other than the actual computer where the passwords reside or were used. Offline attacks usually require physical access to the computer and copying the password file from the system onto removable media. The hacker then takes the file to another computer to perform the cracking. Several types of offline password attacks exist. Table 4.1 illustrates each type of attack:

TABLE 4.1   Offline Attacks

Type of Attack	Characteristics	Example Password
Dictionary attack	Attempts to use passwords from a list of dictionary words	Administrator
Hybrid attack	Substitutes numbers of symbols for password characters	Adm1n1strator
Brute-force attack	Tries all possible combinations of letters, numbers, and special characters	Ms!tr245@F5a

A dictionary attack is the simplest and quickest of type of attack. It's used to identify a password that is an actual word, which can be found in a dictionary. Most commonly, the attack uses a dictionary file of possible words, which is hashed using the same algorithm used by the authentication process. Then, the hashed dictionary words are compared with hashed passwords as the user logs on, or with passwords stored in a file on the server. The dictionary attack works only if the password is an actual dictionary word; therefore this type of attack has some limitations. It can't be used against strong passwords containing numbers or other symbols.

A hybrid attack is the next level of attack a hacker attempts if the password can't be found using a dictionary attack. The hybrid attack starts with a dictionary file and substitutes numbers and symbols for characters in the password. For example, many users add the number 1 to the end of their password to meet strong password requirements. A hybrid attack is designed to find those types of anomalies in passwords.

The most time-consuming type of attack is a brute-force attack, which tries every possible combination of uppercase and lowercase letters, numbers, and symbols. A brute-force attack is the slowest of the three types of attacks because of the many possible combinations of characters in the password. However, brute force is effective; given enough time and processing power, all passwords can eventually be identified.

Nonelectronic Attacks

Nonelectronic—or nontechnical attacks—are attacks that do not employ any technical knowledge. This kind of attack can include social engineering, shoulder surfing, keyboard sniffing and dumpster diving.

Social engineering is the art of interacting with people either face to face or over the telephone and getting them to give out valuable information such as passwords. Social engineering relies on people's good nature and desire to help others. Many times, a help desk is the target of a social-engineering attack because their job is to help people—and recovering or resetting passwords is a common function of the help desk. The best defense against social-engineering attacks is security-awareness training for all employees and security procedures for resetting passwords.

Social engineering was covered in more detail in Chapter 2, "Footprinting and Social Engineering."

Shoulder surfing involves looking over someone's shoulder as they type a password. This can be effective when the hacker is in close proximity to the user and the system. Special screens that make it difficult to see the computer screen from an angle can cut down on shoulder surfing. In addition, employee awareness and training can virtually eliminate this type of attack.

Dumpster diving hackers look through the trash for information such as passwords, which may be written down on a piece of paper. Again, security awareness training on shredding important documents can prevent a hacker from gathering passwords by dumpster diving.

Understanding Keyloggers and Other Spyware Technologies

If all other attempts to gather passwords fail, then a *keystroke logger* is the tool of choice for hackers. Keystroke loggers (keyloggers) can be implemented either using hardware or software. Hardware keyloggers are small hardware devices that connect the keyboard to the PC and save every keystroke into a file or in the memory of the hardware device. In order to install a hardware keylogger, a hacker must have physical access to the system.

Software keyloggers are pieces of stealth software that sit between the keyboard hardware and the operating system, so that they can record every keystroke. Software keyloggers can be deployed on a system by Trojans or viruses.

Using Trojans and viruses will be discussed in Chapter 5, "Trojans, Backdoors, Viruses, and Worms."

Hacking Tools

Spector is spyware that records everything a system does on the Internet, much like a surveillance camera. Spector automatically takes hundreds of snapshots every hour of whatever is on the computer screen and saves these snapshots in a hidden location on the system's hard drive. Spector can be detected and removed with Anti-spector.

eBlaster is Internet spy software that captures incoming and outgoing e-mails and immediately forwards them to another e-mail address. eBlaster can also capture both sides of an Instant Messenger conversation, perform keystroke logging, and record websites visited.

SpyAnywhere is a tool that allows you to view system activity and user actions, shut down/restart, lock down/freeze, and even browse the filesystem of a remote system. SpyAnywhere lets you control open program and windows on the remote system and view Internet histories and related information.

Invisible KeyLogger Stealth (IKS) Software Logger is a high-performance virtual device driver (VxD) that runs silently at the lowest level of the Windows 95/98/ME operating system. All keystrokes are recorded in a binary keystroke file.

Fearless Key Logger is a Trojan that remains resident in memory to capture all user keystrokes. Captured keystrokes are stored in a log file and can be retrieved by a hacker.

E-mail Keylogger logs all e-mails sent and received on a target system. The e-mails can be viewed by sender, recipient, subject, and time/date. The e-mail contents and any attachments are also recorded.

Understand Escalating Privileges

Escalating privileges is the third step in the hacking cycle. *Escalating privileges* basically means adding more rights or permissions to a user account. Simply said, escalating privileges makes a regular user account into an administrator account.

Generally, Administrator accounts have more stringent password requirements, and their passwords are more closely guarded. If it isn't possible to find a username and password of an account with Administrator privileges, then a hacker may choose to use an account with lower privilege. In this case, the hacker must then escalate that account's privileges.

This is accomplished by first gaining access using a nonadmin user account—typically by gathering the username and password through one of the previously discussed methods—and then increasing the privileges on the account to the level of an Administrator.

Once a hacker has a valid user account and password the next step is to execute applications. Generally the hacker needs to have an account with Administrator level access in order to install programs and that is why escalating privileges is so important. In the following sections, we'll see what hackers can do with your system once they have Administrator privileges.

Hacking Tools

GetAdmin.exe is a small program that adds a user to the local administrators group. It uses a low-level NT kernel routine to allowing access to any running process. A logon to the server console is needed to execute the program. GetAdmin.exe is run from the command line or from a browser. It works only with Windows NT 4.0 Service Pack 3.

The Hk.exe utility exposes a Local Procedure Call flaw in Windows NT. A nonadmin user can be escalated to the administrators group using this tool.

Executing Applications

Once a hacker has been able to access an account with Administrator privileges, the next thing they do is execute applications on the target system. The purpose of executing applications may be to install a back door on the system, install a keystroke logger to gather confidential information, copy files, or just cause damage to the system—essentially, anything the hacker wants to do on the system.

Once the hacker is able to execute applications, the system is considered *owned* and under the control of the hacker.

Hacking Tools

PsExec is a program that connects to and executes files on remote systems. No software needs to be installed on the remote system.

Remoxec executes a program using RPC (Task Scheduler) or DCOM (Windows Management Instrumentation) services. Administrators with null or weak passwords may be exploited through Task Scheduler (1025/tcp or above) or Distributed Component Object Mode (DCOM; default 135/tcp).

Buffer Overflows

Buffer overflows are hacking attempts that exploit a flaw in an application's code. Essentially, the buffer overflow attack sends too much information to a field variable in an application, which can cause an application error. Most times, the application doesn't know what action to perform next because it's been overwritten with the overflow data; so it either executes the command in the overflow data or drops out a command prompt to allow the user to enter the next command. The command prompt or shell is the key for a hacker and can be used to execute other applications.

Buffer overflows will be discussed in greater detail in Chapter 9, "SQL Injection and Buffer Overflows."

Understanding Rootkits

A rootkit is a type of program often used to hide utilities on a compromised system. Rootkits include so-called *back doors* to help an attacker subsequently access the system more easily. For example, the rootkit may hide an application that spawns a shell when the attacker connects to a particular network port on the system. A back door may also allow processes started by a nonprivileged user to execute functions normally reserved for the Administrator. A rootkit is frequently used to allow the programmer of the rootkit to see and access usernames and log-in information for sites that require them.

There are several types of rootkits, including the following:

Kernel-level rootkits   Kernel-level rootkits add code and/or replace a portion of kernel code with modified code to help hide a back door on a computer system. This is often accomplished by adding new code to the kernel via a device driver or loadable module, such as loadable kernel modules in Linux or device drivers in Microsoft Windows. Kernel-level rootkits are especially dangerous because they can be difficult to detect without appropriate software.

Library-level rootkits   Library-level rootkits commonly patch, hook, or replace system calls with versions that hide information that might allow the hacker to be identified.

Application-level rootkits   Application-level rootkits may replace regular application binaries with Trojanized fakes, or they may modify the behavior of existing applications using hooks, patches, injected code, or other means.

In the following sections the process of infecting a system with a rootkit will be discussed.

Planting Rootkits on Windows 2000 and XP Machines

The Windows NT/2000 rootkit is built as a kernel mode driver, which can be dynamically loaded at runtime. The rootkit runs with system privileges at the core of the NT kernel, so it has access to all the resources of the operating system. The rootkit can also hide processes, hide files, hide registry entries, intercept keystrokes typed at the system console, issue a debug interrupt to cause a blue screen of death, and redirect EXE files.

The rootkit contains a kernel mode device driver called `_root_.sys` and a launcher program called `DEPLOY.EXE`. After gaining access to the target system, the attacker copies `_root_.sys` and `DEPLOY.EXE` onto the target system and executes `DEPLOY.EXE`. Doing so installs the rootkit device driver and starts it. The attacker later deletes `DEPLOY.EXE` from the target machine. The attacker can then stop and restart the rootkit at will by using the commands `net stop _root_` and `net start _root_`. Once the rootkit is started, the file `_root_.sys` no longer appears in directory listings; the rootkit intercepts system calls for file listings and hides all files beginning with `_root_` from display.

Rootkit Embedded TCP/IP Stack

A new feature of the Windows NT/2000 rootkit is a stateless TCP/IP stack. It works by determining the state of the connection based on the data in the incoming packet. The rootkit has a hard-coded IP address (10.0.0.166) to which it will respond. The rootkit uses raw Ethernet connections to the system's network card, so it's very powerful. The target port doesn't matter; a hacker can telnet to any port on the system. In addition, multiple people can log into the rootkit at once.

Rootkit Countermeasures

All rootkits require administrator access to the target system, so password security is critical. If you detect a rootkit, it's recommended that you back up critical data and reinstall the operating system and applications from a trusted source. The administrator should also keep available a well-documented automated installation procedure and trusted restoration media.

Another countermeasure is to use the *MD5 checksum* utility. The MD5 checksum for a file is a 128-bit value, something like the file's fingerprint. (There is a very small possibility of getting two identical checksums for two different files.) This algorithm is designed so that changing even one bit in the file data causes a different checksum value. This feature can be useful for comparing files and ensuring their integrity. Another good feature is the checksum's fixed length, regardless of the size of the source file.

The MD5 checksum makes sure a file hasn't changed. This can be useful in checking file integrity if a rootkit has been found on a system. Tools such a Tripwire implement MD5 checksums to identify files affected by the rootkit.

Countermeasure Tools

Tripwire is a filesystem integrity-checking program for Unix and Linux operating systems. In addition to one or more cryptographic checksums representing the contents of each directory and file, the Tripwire database also contains information that lets you verify access permissions and file mode settings, the username of the file owner, the date and time the file was last accessed, and the last modification made to the item.

Understanding How to Hide Files

A hacker may want to hide files on a system to prevent their detection. These files may then be used to launch an attack on the system. There are two ways to hide files in Windows. The first is to use the `attrib` command. To hide a file with the `attrib` command, type the following at the command prompt:

```
attrib +h [file/directory]
```

The second way to hide a file in Windows is with NTFS alternate data streaming. NTFS filesystems used by Windows NT, 2000, and XP have a feature called *alternate data streams* that allow data to be stored in hidden files linked to a normal, visible file. Streams aren't limited in size, more than one stream can be linked to a normal file.

NTFS File Streaming

To create and test an NTFS file stream, perform the following steps:

1. At the command line, enter **notepad test.txt**.
2. Put some data in the file, save the file, and close Notepad. Step 1 will open notepad.
3. At the command line, enter **dir test.txt** and note the file size.
4. At the command line, enter **notepad test.txt:hidden.txt**. Type some text into Notepad, save the file, and close it.
5. Check the file size again (it should be the same as in step 3).
6. Open test.txt. You see only the original data.
7. Enter **type test.txt:hidden.txt** at the command line. A syntax error message is displayed.

Hacking Tools

makestrm.exe is a utility that moves the data from a file to an alternate data stream linked to the original file.

NTFS Stream Countermeasures

To delete a stream file, first copy the first file to a FAT partition, and then copy it back to an NTFS partition.

Streams are lost when the file is moved to FAT partition because they're a feature of NTFS and therefore exist only on an NTFS partition.

Countermeasure Tools

You can use LNS.exe to detect NTFS streams. LNS reports the existence and location of files that contain alternate data streams.

Understanding Steganography Technologies

Steganography is the process of hiding data in other types of data such as images or text files. The most popular method of hiding data in files is to utilize graphic images as hiding places. Attackers can embed any information in a graphic file using steganography. The hacker can hide directions on making a bomb, a secret bank account number, or answers to a test. Really any text imaginable can be hidden in an image.

Hacking Tools

ImageHide is a steganography program that hides large amounts of text in images. Even after adding bytes of data, there is no increase in the image size. The image looks the same in a normal graphics programs. It loads and saves to files and therefore is able to bypass most e-mail sniffers.

Blindside is a steganography application that hides information inside BMP (bitmap) images. It's a command-line utility.

MP3Stego hides information in MP3 files during the compression process. The data is compressed, encrypted, and then hidden in the MP3 bit stream.

Snow is a whitespace steganography program that conceals messages in ASCII text by appending whitespace to the end of lines. Because spaces and tabs generally aren't visible in text viewers, the message is effectively hidden from casual observers. If the built-in encryption is used, the message can't be read even if it's detected.

Camera/Shy works with Windows and Internet Explorer and lets users share censored or sensitive information stored in an ordinary GIF image.

Stealth is a filtering tool for PGP files. It strips off identifying information from the header, after which the file can be used for steganography.

Steganography can be detected by some programs, although doing so is difficult. The first step in detection is to locate files with hidden text, which can be done by analyzing patterns in the images and changes to the color palette.

Countermeasure Tools

Stegdetect is an automated tool for detecting steganographic content in images. It's capable of detecting different steganographic methods to embed hidden information in JPEG images.

Dskprobe is a tool on the Windows 2000 installation CD. It's a low-level hard-disk scanner that can detect steganography.

Understanding How to Cover Your Tracks and Erase Evidence

Once intruders have successfully gained Administrator access on a system, they try to cover their tracks to prevent detection of their presence (either current or past) on the system. A hacker may also try to remove evidence of their identity or activities on the system to prevent tracing of their identity or location by authorities. The hacker usually erases any error messages or security events that have been logged, to prevent detection.

In the following sections, we'll look at disabling auditing and clearing the event log, which are two methods used by a hacker to cover their tracks and avoid detection.

Disabling Auditing

The first thing intruders do after gaining Administrator privileges is to disable auditing. Windows auditing records certain events in a log file that is stored in the Windows Event Viewer. Events can include logging in to the system, an application, or an event log. An administrator can choose the level of logging implemented on a system. A hacker wants to determine the level of logging implemented to see whether they need to clear events that indicate their presence on the system.

Hacking Tools

AuditPol is a tool included in the Windows NT Resource Kit for system administrators. This tool can disable or enable auditing from the Windows command line. It can also be used to determine the level of logging implemented by a systems administrator.

Clearing the Event Log

Intruders can easily wipe out the security logs in the Windows Event Viewer. An event log that contains one or few events is suspicious because it usually indicates that other events have been cleared. It's still necessary to clear the event log after disabling auditing, because using the Audit-Pol tool places an entry in the event log indicating that auditing has been disabled. Several tools exist to clear the event log, or a hacker can do so manually in the Windows Event Viewer.

Hacking Tools

The elsave.exe utility is a simple tool for clearing the event log. It's command-line based.

WinZapper is a tool that an attacker can use to erase event records selectively from the security log in Windows 2000. WinZapper also ensures that no security events are logged while the program is running.

Evidence Eliminator is a data-cleansing system for Windows PCs. It prevents unwanted data from becoming permanently hidden in the system. It cleans the recycle bin, Internet cache, system files, temp folders, and so on. Evidence Eliminator can also be used by a hacker to remove evidence from a system after an attack.

Exam Essentials

Understand the importance of password security.   Implementing password-change intervals, strong alphanumeric passwords, and other password security measures is critical to network security.

Know the different types of password attacks.   Passive online attacks include sniffing, man-in-the-middle, and replay. Active online attacks include passive and automated password guessing. Offline attacks include dictionary, hybrid, and brute force. Nonelectronic attacks include shoulder surfing, keyboard sniffing, and social engineering.

Understand the different types of offline password attacks.   Dictionary, hybrid, and brute-force attacks are all offline password attacks.

Know the ways to defend against password guessing.   Smart cards and biometrics are two ways to increase security and defend against password guessing.

Understand the differences between the types of nonelectronic attacks.   Social engineering, shoulder surfing, and dumpster diving are all types of nonelectronic attacks.

Know how evidence of hacking activity is eliminated by attackers.   Clearing event logs and disabling auditing are methods that attackers use to cover their tracks.

Realize that hiding files are means used to sneak out sensitive information.   Steganography, NTFS streaming, and the attrib command are all ways hackers can hide and steal files.

Review Questions

1. What is the process of hiding text within an image called?

    A. Steganography

    B. Encryption

    C. Spyware

    D. Keystroke logging

2. What is a rootkit?

    A. A simple tool to gain access to the root of the Windows system

    B. A Trojan that sends information to an SMB relay

    C. An invasive program that affects the system files, including the kernel and libraries

    D. A tool to perform a buffer overflow

3. Why would hackers want to cover their tracks?

    A. To prevent another person from using the programs they have installed on a target system

    B. To prevent detection or discovery

    C. To prevent hacking attempts

    D. To keep other hackers from using their tools

4. What is privilege escalation?

    A. Creating a user account with higher privileges

    B. Creating a user account with Administrator privileges

    C. Creating two user accounts: one with high privileges and one with lower privileges

    D. Increasing privileges on a user account

5. What are two methods used to hide files? (Choose all that apply.)

    A. NTFS file streaming

    B. `Attrib` command

    C. Steganography

    D. Encrypted File System

6. What is the recommended password-change interval?

    A. 30 days

    B. 20 days

    C. 1 day

    D. 7 days

7. What type of password attack would be most successful against the password T63k#s23A?

  A. Dictionary

  B. Hybrid

  C. Password guessing

  D. Brute force

8. Which of the following is a passive online attack?

  A. Password guessing

  B. Network sniffing

  C. Brute-force attack

  D. Dictionary attack

9. Why is it necessary to clear the event log after using the `auditpol` command to turn off logging?

  A. The `auditpol` command places an entry in the event log.

  B. The `auditpol` command doesn't stop logging until the event log has been cleared.

  C. `auditpol` relies on the event log to determine whether logging is taking place.

  D. The event log doesn't need to be cleared after running the `auditpol` command.

10. What is necessary in order to install a hardware keylogger on a target system?

  A. The IP address of the system

  B. The Administrator username and password

  C. Physical access to the system

  D. Telnet access to the system

Answers to Review Questions

1. A. Steganography is the process of hiding text within an image.

2. C. A rootkit is a program that modifies the core of the operating system: the kernel and libraries.

3. B. Hackers cover their tracks to keep from having their identity or location discovered.

4. D. Privilege escalation is a hacking method to increase privileges on a user account.

5. A, B. NTFS file streaming and the `attrib` command are two hacking techniques to hide files.

6. A. Passwords should be changed every 30 days for the best balance of security and usability.

7. D. A brute-force attack tries every combination of letters, numbers, and symbols.

8. B. Network sniffing is a passive online attack because it can't be detected.

9. A. The event log must be cleared because the `auditpol` command places an entry in the event log indicating that login has been disabled.

10. C. A hardware keylogger is an adapter that connects the keyboard to the PC. A hacker needs physical access to the PC in order to plug in the hardware keylogger.

Chapter 5

Trojans, Backdoors, Viruses, and Worms

CEH EXAM OBJECTIVES COVERED IN THIS CHAPTER:

✓ **Trojans and Backdoors**

- What Is a Trojan?
- What Is Meant by Overt and Covert channels?
- List the Different Types of Trojans
- How Do Reverse-Connecting Trojans Work?
- Understand How the Netcat Trojan Works
- What Are the Indications of a Trojan Attack?
- What Is Meant by "Wrapping"?
- What Are the Countermeasure Techniques Used to Prevent Trojans?
- Understand Trojan Evading Techniques

✓ **Viruses and Worms**

- Understand the Differences between a Virus and a Worm
- Understand the Types of Viruses
- How a Virus Spreads and Infects a System
- Understand Antivirus Evasion Techniques
- Understand Virus Detection Methods

Trojans and backdoors are two ways a hacker can gain access to a target system. They come in many different varieties, but they all have one thing in common: They must be installed by another program, or the user must be tricked into installing the Trojan or backdoor on their system. Trojans and backdoors are potentially harmful tools in the ethical hacker's toolkit and should be used judiciously to test the security of a system or network.

Viruses and worms can be just as destructive to systems and networks as Trojans and backdoors. In fact, many viruses carry Trojan executables and can infect a system then create a backdoor for hackers. This chapter will discuss the similarities and differences among Trojans, backdoors, viruses, and worms. All of these types of malicious code or malware are important to ethical hackers because they are commonly used by hackers to attack compromised systems.

Trojans and Backdoors

A *backdoor* is a program or a set of related programs that a hacker installs on a target system to allow access to the system at a later time. A backdoor's goal is to remove the evidence of initial entry from the system's log files. But a backdoor may also let a hacker retain access to a machine it has penetrated even if the intrusion has already been detected and remedied by the system administrator.

Adding a new service is the most common technique to disguise backdoors in the Windows operating system. Before the installation of a backdoor, a hacker must investigate the system to find services that are running. The hacker could add a new service and give it an inconspicuous name or better yet choose a service that's never used and that is either activated manually or completely disabled.

This technique is effective because when a hacking attempt occurs the system administrator usually focuses on looking for something odd in the system, leaving all existing services unchecked. The backdoor technique is simple but efficient: The hacker can get back into the machine with the least amount of visibility in the server logs. The backdoored service lets the hacker use higher privileges—in most cases, as a System account.

Remote Administration Trojans (RATs) are a class of backdoors used to enable remote control over a compromised machine. They provide apparently useful functions to the user and, at the same time, open a network port on the victim computer. Once the RAT is started, it behaves as an executable file, interacting with certain registry keys responsible for starting processes and sometimes creating its own system services. Unlike common backdoors, RATs hook themselves into the victim operating system and always come packaged with two files: the client file and the server file. The server is installed in the infected machine, and the client is used by the intruder to control the compromised system.

What Is a Trojan?

A *Trojan* is a malicious program disguised as something benign. Trojans are often downloaded along with another program or software package. Once installed on a system, they can cause data theft and loss, and system crashes or slowdowns; they can also be used as launching points for other attacks such as Distributed Denial of Service (DDOS). Many Trojans are used to manipulate files on the victim computer, manage processes, remotely run commands, intercept keystrokes, watch screen images, and restart or shut down infected hosts. Sophisticated Trojans can connect themselves to their originator or announce the Trojan infection on an Internet Relay Chat (IRC) channel.

Trojans ride on the backs of other programs and are usually installed on a system without the user's knowledge. A Trojan can be sent to a victim system in many ways: as an Instant Messenger (IM) attachment, IRC, an e-mail attachment, or NetBIOS file sharing. Many fake programs purporting to be legitimate software such as freeware, spyware-removal tools, system optimizers, screen savers, music, pictures, games, and videos can install a Trojan on a system just by being downloaded. Advertisements for free programs, music files, or video files lure a victim into installing the Trojan program; the program then has system-level access on the target system, where it can be destructive and insidious.

Table 5.1 lists some common Trojans and their default port numbers.

TABLE 5.1   Common Trojan Programs

Trojan	Protocol	Port
BackOrifice	UDP	31337 or 31338
Deep Throat	UDP	2140 and 3150
NetBus	TCP	12345 and 12346
Whack-a-mole	TCP	12361 and 12362
NetBus 2	TCP	20034
GirlFriend	TCP	21544
Masters Paradise	TCP	3129, 40421, 40422, 40423, and 40426

What Is Meant by Overt and Covert Channels?

An *overt channel* is the normal and a legitimate way that programs communicate within a computer system or network. A *covert channel* uses programs or communications paths in ways that were not intended.

Trojans can use covert channels to communicate. Some client Trojans use covert channels to send instructions to the server component on the compromised system. This sometimes makes Trojan communication difficult to decipher and understand.

Covert channels rely on a technique called *tunneling*, which lets one protocol be carried over another protocol. Internet Control Message Protocol (ICMP) tunneling is a method of using ICMP echo-request and echo-reply to carry any payload an attacker may wish to use, in an attempt to stealthily access or control a compromised system.

Hacking Tool

Loki is a hacking tool that provides shell access over ICMP, making it much more difficult to detect than TCP- or UDP-based backdoors. As far as the network is concerned, a series of ICMP packets is being sent across the network. However, the hacker is really sending commands from the Loki client and executing them on the server.

List the Different Types of Trojans

Trojans can be created and used to perform different attacks. Some of the most common types of Trojans are:

- Remote Access Trojans (RATs)—used to gain remote access to a system
- Data-Sending Trojans—used to find data on a system and deliver data to a hacker
- Destructive Trojans—used to delete or corrupt files on a system
- Denial of Service Trojans—used to launch a denial or service attack
- Proxy Trojans—used to tunnel traffic or launch hacking attacks via other system
- FTP Trojans—used to create an FTP server in order to copy files onto a system
- Security software disabler Trojans—used to stop antivirus software

How Do Reverse-Connecting Trojans Work?

Reverse-connecting Trojans let an attacker access a machine on the internal network from the outside. The hacker can install a simple Trojan program on a system on the internal network, such as the reverse WWW shell server. On a regular basis (usually every 60 seconds), the internal server tries to access the external master system to pick up commands. If the attacker has typed something into the master system, this command is retrieved and executed on the internal system. Reverse WWW shell uses standard HTTP. It's dangerous because it's difficult to detect—it looks like a client is browsing the Web from the internal network.

Hacking Tools

TROJ_QAZ is a Trojan that renames the application `notepad.exe` file to `note.com` and then copies itself as `notepad.exe` to the Windows folder. This will cause the Trojan to be launched every time a user runs Notepad. It has a backdoor that a remote user or hacker can use to connect to and control the computer using port 7597. TROJ_QAZ also infects the registry so that it is loaded every time Windows is started.

Tini is a very small and simple backdoor Trojan for Windows operating systems. It listens on port 7777 and gives a hacker a remote command prompt on the target system. To connect to a Tini server, the hacker telnets to port 7777.

Donald Dick is a backdoor Trojan for Windows OS's that allows a hacker full access to a system over the Internet. The hacker can read, write, delete, or run any program on the system. Donald Dick also includes a keylogger and a registry parser and can perform functions such as opening or closing the CD-ROM tray. The attacker uses the client to send commands the victim listening on a predefined port. Donald Dick uses default port 23476 or 23477.

NetBus is a Windows GUI Trojan program and is similar in functionality to Donald Dick. It adds the registry key `HKEY_CURRENT_USER\NetBus Server` and modifies the `HKEY_CURRENT_USER\NetBus Server\General\TCPPort` key. If NetBus is configured to start automatically, it adds a registry entry called NetBus Server Pro in `HKEY_LOCAL_MACHINE\Software\Microsoft\Windows\CurrentVersion\RunServices`.

SubSeven is a Trojan that can be configured to notify a hacker when the infected computer connects to the Internet and can tell the hacker information about the system. This notification can be done over an IRC network, by ICQ, or by e-mail. SubSeven can cause a system to slow down, and generates error messages on the infected system.

BackOrifice 2000 is a remote administration tool that an attacker can use to control a system across a TCP/IP connection using a GUI interface. BackOrifice doesn't appear in the task list or list of processes, and it copies itself into the registry to run every time the computer is started. The filename that it runs is configurable before it's installed. BackOrifice modifies the `HKEY_LOCAL_MACHINE\SOFTWARE\Microsoft\Windows\CurrentVersion\RunServices` registry key. BackOrifice plug-ins add features to the BackOrifice program. Plug-ins include cryptographically strong Triple DES encryption, a remote desktop with optional mouse and keyboard control, drag-and-drop encrypted file transfers, Explorer-like filesystem browsing, graphical remote registry editing, reliable UDP and ICMP communications protocols, and stealth capabilities that are achieved by using ICMP instead of TCP and UDP.

BoSniffer appears to be a fix for BackOrifice but is actually a BackOrifice server with the SpeakEasy plug-in installed. If `BoSniffer.exe`, the BoSniffer executable, is run on a target system it attempts to log on to a predetermined IRC server on channel `#BO_OWNED` with a random username. It then proceeds to announce its IP address and a custom message every few minutes so that the hacker community can use this system as a zombie for future attacks.

ComputerSpy Key Logger is a program that a hacker can use to record computer activities on a computer, such as websites visited; logins and passwords for ICQ, MSN, AOL, AIM, and Yahoo Messenger or webmail; current applications that are running or executed; Internet chats; and e-mail. The program can even take snapshots of the entire Windows desktop at set intervals.

Beast is a Trojan that runs in the memory allocated for the WinLogon.exe service. Once installed, the program inserts itself into Windows Explorer or Internet Explorer. One of Beast's most distinct features is that it's an all-in-one Trojan, meaning the client, the server, and the server editor are stored in the same application.

CyberSpy is a Telnet Trojan that copies itself into the Windows system directory and registers itself in the system registry so that it starts each time an infected system is rebooted. Once this is done, it sends a notice via e-mail or ICQ and then begins to listen to a previously specified TCP/IP port.

SubRoot is a remote administration Trojan that a hacker can use to connect to a victim system on TCP port 1700.

LetMeRule is a remote access Trojan that can be configured to listen on any port on a target system. It includes a command prompt that an attacker uses to control the target system. It can delete all files in a specific director, execute files at the remote host, or view and modify the registry.

Firekiller 2000 disables antivirus programs and software firewalls. For instance, if Norton Anti-Virus is in auto scan mode in the Taskbar, and ATGuard Firewall is activated, the program stops both on execution and makes the installations of both unusable on the hard drive. They must then be reinstalled to restore their functionality. Firekiller 2000 works with all major protection software, including ATGuard, Conseal, Norton Anti-Virus, and McAfee Antivirus.

The Hard Drive Killer Pro programs offer the ability to fully and permanently destroy all data on any given DOS or Windows system. The program, once executed, deletes files and infects and reboots the system within a few seconds. After rebooting, all hard drives attached to the system are formatted in an unrecoverable manner within only 1 to 2 seconds, regardless of the size of the hard drive.

Understand How the Netcat Trojan Works

Netcat is a Trojan that uses a command-line interface to open TCP or UDP ports on a target system. A hacker can then telnet to those open ports and gain shell access to the target system.

    For the CEH exam, it's important to know how to use Netcat. Make sure you download the Netcat tool and practice the commands before attempting the exam.

What Are the Indications of a Trojan Attack?

Unusual system behavior is usually an indication of a Trojan attack. Actions such as programs starting and running without the user's initiation; CD-ROM drawers opening or closing; wallpaper, background, or screen saver settings changing by themselves; the screen display flipping upside down; and a browser program opening strange or unexpected websites are all indications of a Trojan attack. Any action that is suspicious or not initiated by the user can be an indication of a Trojan attack.

What Is Meant by "Wrapping"?

Wrappers are software packages that can be used to deliver a Trojan. The wrapper binds a legitimate file to the Trojan file. Both the legitimate software and the Trojan are combined into a single executable file and installed when the program is run.

Generally, games or other animated installations are used as wrappers because they entertain the user while the Trojan in being installed. This way, the user doesn't notice the slower processing that occurs while the Trojan is being installed on the system—the user only sees the legitimate application being installed.

Hacking Tools

Graffiti is an animated game that can be wrapped with a Trojan. It entertains the user with an animated game while the Trojan is being installed in the background.

Silk Rope 2000 is a wrapper that combines the BackOrifice server and any other specified application.

ELiTeWrap is an advanced .exe wrapper for Windows used for installing and running programs. ELiTeWrap can create a setup program to extract files to a directory and execute programs or batch files that display help menus or copy files on to the target system.

IconPlus is a conversion program that translates icons between various formats. An attacker can use this type of application to disguise malicious code or a Trojan so that users are tricked into executing it thinking it is a legitimate application.

Trojan Construction Kit and Trojan Makers

Several Trojan-generator tools enable hackers to create their own Trojans. Such toolkits help hackers construct Trojans that can be customized. These tools can be dangerous and can backfire if not executed properly. New Trojans created by hackers usually have the added benefit of passing undetected through virus-scanning and Trojan-scanning tools because they don't match any know signatures.

Some of the Trojan kits available in the wild are Senna Spy Generator, the Trojan Horse Construction Kit v2.0, Progenic Mail Trojan Construction Kit, and Pandora's Box.

What Are the Countermeasure Techniques in Preventing Trojans?

Most commercial antivirus program have anti-Trojan capabilities as well as spyware detection and removal functionality. These tools can automatically scan hard drives on startup to detect backdoor and Trojan programs before they can cause damage. Once a system is infected, it's more difficult to clean, but you can do so with commercially available tools.

It's important to use commercial applications to clean a system instead of freeware tools, because many freeware removal tools can further infect the system. In addition, port-monitoring tools can identify ports that have been opened or files that have changed.

Understand Trojan-Evading Techniques

The key to preventing Trojans and backdoors from being installed on a system is to educate users not to install applications downloaded from the Internet or open e-mail attachments from parties they don't know. Many systems administrators don't give users the system permissions necessary to install programs on their system for that very reason.

Port-Monitoring and Trojan-Detection Tools

Fport reports all open TCP/IP and UDP ports and maps them to the owning application. You can use fport to quickly identify unknown open ports and their associated applications.

TCPView is a Windows program that shows detailed listings of all TCP and UDP endpoints on the system, including the local and remote addresses and state of TCP connections. When TCPView runs, it enumerates all active TCP and UDP endpoints, resolving all IP addresses to their domain-name versions.

PrcView is a process viewer utility that displays detailed information about processes running under Windows. PrcView comes with a command-line version you can use to write scripts that check whether a process is running and, if so, kill it.

Inzider is a useful tool that lists processes in the Windows system and the ports on which each one listens. Inzider may pick up some Trojans. For instance, BackOrifice injects itself into other processes, so it isn't visible in the Task Manager as a separate process, but it does have an open port that it listens on.

Tripwire verifies system integrity. It automatically calculates cryptographic hashes of all key system files or any file that is to be monitored for modifications. The Tripwire software works by creating a baseline snapshot of the system. It periodically scans those files, recalculates the information, and sees whether any of the information has changed. If there is a change, an alarm is raised.

Dsniff is a collection of tools used for network auditing and penetration testing. Dsniff, filesnarf, mailsnarf, msgsnarf, urlsnarf, and WebSpy passively monitor a network for interesting data such as passwords, e-mail, and file transfers. Arpspoof, dnsspoof, and macof facilitate the interception of network traffic normally unavailable to an attacker due to layer 2 switching. Sshmitm and webmitm implement active man-in-the-middle attacks against redirected Secure Shell (SSH) and HTTP Over SSL (HTTPS) sessions by exploiting weak bindings in ad hoc Public Key Infrastructure (PKI). These tools will be discussed in further detail in Chapter 6, "Sniffers."

System File Verification Subobjective to Trojan Countermeasures

Windows 2003 includes a feature called Windows File Protection (WFP) that prevents the replacement of protected files. WFP checks the file integrity when an attempt is made to overwrite a SYS, DLL, OCX, TTF, or EXE file. This ensures that only Microsoft verified files are used to replace system files.

Another tool called sigverif checks to see what files Microsoft has digitally signed on a system. To run sigverif, perform the following steps:

1. Click the Start button.
2. Click Run.
3. Type **sigverif**, and click Start. The results will be displayed.

System File Checker is another command-line–based tool used to check whether a Trojan program has replaced files. If System File Checker detects that a file has been overwritten, it retrieves a known good file from the `Windows\system32\dllcache` folder and overwrites the unverified file. The command to run the System File Checker is `sfc/scannow`.

Viruses and Worms

Viruses and worms can be used to infect a system and modify a system to allow a hacker to gain access. Many viruses and worms carry Trojans and backdoors. In this way a virus or worm is a carrier and allows malicious code such as Trojans and backdoors to be transferred from system to system much in the way that contact between people allows germs to spread.

Understand the Difference between a Virus and a Worm

A *virus* and a *worm* are similar in that they're both forms of malicious software (*malware*). A virus infects another executable and uses this carrier program to spread itself. The virus code is injected into the previously benign program and is spread when the program is run. Examples of virus carrier programs are macros, games, e-mail attachments, Visual Basic scripts, games, and animations.

A worm is a type of virus, but it's self-replicating. A worm spreads from system to system automatically, but a virus needs another program in order to spread. Viruses and worms both execute without the knowledge or desire of the end user.

Understand the Types of Viruses

Viruses are classified according to two factors: what they infect and how they infect. A virus can infect the following components of a system:

- System sectors
- Files
- Macros (such as Microsoft Word macros)
- Companion files (supporting system files like DLL and INI files)
- Disk clusters
- Batch files (BAT files)
- Source code

How a Virus Spreads and Infects the System

A virus infects through interaction with an outside system. Viruses are categorized according to their infection technique, as follows:

Polymorphic viruses   These viruses encrypt the code in a different way with each infection and can change to different forms to try to evade detection.

Stealth viruses   These hide the normal virus characteristics, such as modifying the original time and date stamp of the file so as to prevent the virus from being noticed as a new file on the system.

Fast and slow infectors   These can evade detection by infecting very quickly or very slowly.

Sparse infectors   These viruses infect only a few systems or applications.

Armored viruses   These are encrypted to prevent detection.

Multipartite viruses   These advanced viruses create multiple infections.

Cavity (space-filler) viruses   These viruses attach to empty areas of files.

Tunneling viruses   These are sent via a different protocol or encrypted to prevent detection or allow it to pass through a firewall.

Camouflage viruses   These viruses appear to be another program.

NTFS and Active Directory viruses   These specifically attack the NT file system or Active Directory on Windows systems.

Understand Antivirus Evasion Techniques

An attacker can write a custom script or virus that won't be detected by antivirus programs. Virus detection and removal is based on a signature of the program. Until the virus is detected and antivirus companies have a chance to update virus definitions, the virus goes undetected. This allows an attacker to evade antivirus detection and removal for a period of time.

Understand Virus Detection Methods

The following techniques are used to detect viruses:

- Scanning
- Integrity checking with checksums
- Interception based on a virus signature

The process of virus detection and removal is as follows:

1. Detect the attack as a virus. Not all anomalous behavior can be attributed to a virus.

2. Trace processes using utilities such as `handle.exe`, `listdlls.exe`, `fport.exe`, `netstat.exe`, and `pslist.exe`, and map commonalities between affected systems.

3. Detect the virus payload by looking for altered, replaced, or deleted files. New files, changed file attributes, or shared library files should be checked.

4. Acquire the infection vector and isolate it. Then, update your antivirus definitions and rescan all systems.

A test virus can be created by typing the following code in Notepad and saving the file as `EICAR.COM`. Your antivirus program should respond when you attempt to open, run, or copy it.

X5O!P%@AP[4\PZX54(P^)7CC)7}$EICAR-STANDARD-ANTIVIRUS-TEST-FILE!$H+H*

Exam Essentials

Understand the definition of a Trojan.   Trojans are malicious pieces of code that are carried by software to a target system.

Understand the definition of a covert channel.   A covert channel uses communications in a way that was not intended.

Understand common covert channels   ICMP tunneling, reverse WWW shell, and man-in-the-middle attacks are common covert channels.

Understand the definition of a backdoor.   A backdoor is usually a component of a Trojan. It's used to maintain access after the initial system weakness has been discovered and removed. It usually takes the form of a port being opened on a compromised system.

Understand the use of a Trojan.   Trojans are used primarily to gain and retain access on the target system.

Understand how Trojans work.   A Trojan often resides deep in the system and makes registry changes that allow it to meet its purpose as a remote administration tool.

Know the best Trojan countermeasures.   Awareness and preventive measures are the best defenses against Trojans.

Understand how a virus is different from a worm.   Viruses must attach themselves to other programs, whereas worms spread automatically.

Understand the different types of viruses   Polymorphic, stealth, fast infectors, slow infectors, sparse infectors, armored, multipartite, cavity, tunneling, camouflage, NTFS, and AD viruses are all types of viruses.

Review Questions

1. What is a wrapper?

   A. A Trojaned system

   B. A program used to combine a Trojan and legitimate software into a single executable

   C. A program used to combine a Trojan and a backdoor into a single executable

   D. A way of accessing a Trojaned system

2. What is the difference between a backdoor and a Trojan?

   A. A Trojan usually provides a backdoor for a hacker.

   B. A backdoor must be installed first.

   C. A Trojan is not a way to access a system.

   D. A backdoor is provided only through a virus, not through a Trojan.

3. What port does Tini use by default?

   A. 12345

   B. 71

   C. 7777

   D. 666

4. Which is the best Trojan and backdoor countermeasure?

   A. Scan the hard drive on network connection, and educate users not to install unknown software.

   B. Implement a network firewall.

   C. Implement personal firewall software.

   D. Educate systems administrators about the risks of using systems without firewalls.

   E. Scan the hard drive on startup.

5. How do you remove a Trojan from a system?

   A. Search the Internet for freeware removal tools.

   B. Purchase commercially available tools to remove the Trojan.

   C. Reboot the system.

   D. Uninstall and reinstall all applications.

6. What is ICMP tunneling?

   A. Tunneling ICMP messages through HTTP

   B. Tunneling another protocol through ICMP

   C. An overt channel

   D. Sending ICMP commands using a different protocol

7. What is reverse WWW shell?

    A. Connecting to a website using a tunnel

    B. A Trojan that connects from the server to the client using HTTP

    C. A Trojan that issues command to the client using HTTP

    D. Connecting through a firewall

8. What is a covert channel?

    A. Using a communications channel in a way that was not intended

    B. Tunneling software

    C. A Trojan removal tool

    D. Using a communications channel in the original, intended way

9. What is the purpose of system-file verification?

    A. To find system files

    B. To determine whether system files have been changed or modified

    C. To find out if a backdoor has been installed

    D. To remove a Trojan

10. Which of the following is an example of a covert channel?

    A. Reverse WWW shell

    B. Firewalking

    C. SNMP enumeration

    D. Steganography

11. What is the difference between a virus and a worm?

    A. A virus can infect the boot sector but a worm cannot.

    B. A worm spreads by itself but a virus must attach to an e-mail.

    C. A worm spreads by itself but a virus must attach to another program.

    D. A virus is written in C++ but a worm is written in shell code.

12. What type of virus modifies itself to avoid detection?

    A. Stealth virus

    B. Polymorphic virus

    C. Multipartite virus

    D. Armored virus

13. Which virus spreads through Word macros?

    A. Melissa

    B. Slammer

    C. Sobig

    D. Blaster

14. Which worm affects SQL servers?

   A. Sobig

   B. SQL Blaster

   C. SQL Slammer

   D. Melissa

15. Armored viruses are _____.

   A. Hidden

   B. Tunneled

   C. Encrypted

   D. Stealth

16. What are the three methods used to detect a virus?

   A. Scanning

   B. Integrity checking

   C. Virus signature comparison

   D. Firewall rules

   E. IDS anomaly detection

   F. Sniffing

17. What components of a system do viruses infect?

   A. Files

   B. System sectors

   C. Memory

   D. CPU

   E. DLL files

18. All anomalous behavior can be attributed to a virus.

   A. True

   B. False

19. A virus that can cause multiple infections is know as what type of virus?

   A. Multipartite

   B. Stealth

   C. Camouflage

   D. Multi-infection

20. A way to evade an antivirus program is to do what?

   A. Write a custom virus script.

   B. Write a custom virus signature.

   C. Write a custom virus evasion program.

   D. Write a custom virus detection program.

Answers to Review Questions

1. B. A wrapper is software used to combine a Trojan and legitimate software into a single executable so that the Trojan is installed during the installation of the other software.

2. A. A Trojan infects a system first and usually includes a backdoor for later access.

3. C. Tini uses port 7777 by default.

4. A. The best prevention is to scan the hard drive for known Trojans on network connection and backdoors and to educate users not to install any unknown software.

5. B. To remove a Trojan, you should use commercial tools. Many freeware tools contain Trojans.

6. B. ICMP tunneling involves sending what appear to be ICMP commands but really are Trojan communications.

7. B. Reverse WWW shell is a connection from a Trojan server component on the compromised system to the Trojan client on the hacker's system.

8. A. A covert channel is the use of a protocol or communications channel in a nontraditional way.

9. B. System-file verification tracks changes made to system files and ensures that a Trojan has not overwritten a critical system file.

10. A. Reverse WWW shell is an example of a covert channel.

11. C. A worm can replicate itself automatically but a virus must attach to another program.

12. B. A polymorphic virus modifies itself to evade detection.

13. A. Melissa is a virus that spreads via Word Macros.

14. C. SQL Slammer is a worm that attacks SQL servers.

15. C. Armored viruses are encrypted.

16. A, B, C. Scanning, integrity checking, and virus signature comparison are three ways to detect a virus infection.

17. A, B, E. A virus can affect files, system sectors, and DLL files.

18. False. Not all anomalous behavior can be attributed to a virus.

19. A. A multipartite virus can cause multiple infections.

20. A. A custom virus script can be used to evade detection because the script will not match a virus signature.

Chapter

6

Sniffers

CEH EXAM OBJECTIVES COVERED IN THIS CHAPTER:

- ✓ Understand the Protocols Susceptible to Sniffing
- ✓ Understand Active and Passive Sniffing
- ✓ Understand ARP Poisoning
- ✓ Understand Ethereal Capture and Display Filters
- ✓ Understand MAC Flooding
- ✓ Understand DNS Spoofing Techniques
- ✓ Describe Sniffing Countermeasures

A *sniffer* can be a packet-capturing or frame-capturing tool. It intercepts traffic on the network and displays it in either a command-line or GUI format for a hacker to view. Some sophisticated sniffers interpret the packets and can reassemble the packet stream into the original data, such as an e-mail or a document.

Sniffers are used to capture traffic sent between two systems. Depending on how the sniffer is used and the security measures in place, a hacker can use a sniffer to discover usernames, passwords, and other confidential information transmitted on the network. Several hacking attacks and various hacking tools require the use of a sniffer to obtain important information sent from the target system. This chapter will describe how sniffers work and identify the most common sniffer hacking tools.

The term *packet* refers to the data at layer 3 or the network layer of the OSI model whereas *frame* refers to data at layer 2 or the data link layer. Frames contain MAC addresses, and packets contain IP addresses.

Understand the Protocols Susceptible to Sniffing

Sniffer software works by capturing packets not destined for the system's MAC address but rather for a target's destination MAC address. This is known as *promiscuous mode*. Normally, a system on the network reads and responds only to traffic sent directly to its MAC address. In promiscuous mode, the system reads all traffic and sends it to the sniffer for processing. Promiscuous mode is enabled on a network card with the installation of special driver software. Many of the hacking tools for sniffing include a promiscuous-mode driver to facilitate this process.

Any protocols that don't encrypt data are susceptible to sniffing. Protocols such as HTTP, POP3, Simple Network Management Protocol (SNMP), and FTP are most commonly captured using a sniffer and viewed by a hacker to gather valuable information such as usernames and passwords.

Hacking Tools

Ethereal is a freeware sniffer that can capture packets from a wired or wireless LAN connection. The latest version has been renamed WireShark. Ethereal is a common and popular program because it is free but has some drawbacks. An untrained user may find it difficult to write filters in Ethereal to capture only certain types of traffic.

Snort is an intrusion detection system (IDS) that also has sniffer capabilities. It can be used to detect a variety of attacks and probes, such as buffer overflows, stealth port scans, CGI attacks, Server Message Block (SMB) probes, and OS fingerprinting attempts.

WinDump is the Windows version of tcpdump, the command-line network analyzer for Unix. WinDump is fully compatible with tcpdump and can be used to watch, diagnose, and save to disk network traffic according to various rules.

EtherPeek is a great sniffer for wired networks with extensive filtering and TCP/IP conversation tracking capabilities. The latest version of EtherPeek has been renamed OmniPeek.

WinSniffer is an efficient password sniffer. It monitors incoming and outgoing network traffic and decodes FTP, POP3, HTTP, ICQ, Simple Mail Transfer Protocol (SMTP), Telnet, Internet Message Access Protocol (IMAP), and Network News Transfer Protocol (NNTP) usernames and passwords.

Iris is an advanced data- and network-traffic analyzer that collects, stores, organizes, and reports all data traffic on a network. Unlike other network sniffers, Iris is able to reconstruct network traffic, such as graphics, documents, and e-mails including attachments.

Understand Active and Passive Sniffing

There are two different types of sniffing: passive and active. *Passive sniffing* involves listening and capturing traffic, and is useful in a network connected by hubs; *active sniffing* involves launching an Address Resolution Protocol (ARP) spoofing or traffic-flooding attack against a switch in order to capture traffic. As the names indicate, active sniffing is detectable but passive sniffing isn't.

In networks that use hubs or wireless media to connect systems, all hosts on the network can see all traffic; therefore a passive packet sniffer can capture traffic going to and from all hosts connected via the hub. A switched network operates differently. The switch looks at the data sent to it and tries to forward packets to their intended recipients based on MAC address. The switch maintains a MAC table of all the systems and the port numbers to which they're connected. This enables the switch to segment the network traffic and send traffic only to the correct destination MAC addresses. A switch network has greatly improved throughput and is more secure than a shared network connected via hubs.

Understand ARP Poisoning

ARP allows the network to translate IP addresses into MAC addresses. When one host using TCP/IP on a LAN tries to contact another, it needs the MAC address or hardware address of the host it's trying to reach. It first looks in its ARP cache to see if it already has the MAC address; if it doesn't, it broadcasts an ARP request asking, "Who has the IP address I'm looking for?" If the host that has that IP address hears the ARP query, it responds with its own MAC address, and a conversation can begin using TCP/IP.

ARP poisoning is a technique that's used to attack an Ethernet network and that may let an attacker sniff data frames on a switched LAN or stop the traffic altogether. ARP poisoning utilizes ARP spoofing where the purpose is to send fake, or spoofed, ARP messages to an Ethernet LAN. These frames contain false MAC addresses that confuse network devices such as network switches. As a result, frames intended for one machine can be mistakenly sent to another (allowing the packets to be sniffed) or to an unreachable host (a Denial of Service [DoS] attack). ARP spoofing can also be used in a man-in-the-middle attack in which all traffic is forwarded through a host by means of ARP spoofing and analyzed for passwords and other information.

To prevent ARP spoofing, permanently add the MAC address of the gateway to the ARP cache on a system. You can do this on a Windows system by using the `ARP -s` command at the command line and appending the gateway's IP and MAC addresses. Doing so prevents a hacker from overwriting the ARP cache to perform ARP spoofing on the system but can be difficult to manage in a large environment because of the number of systems. In an enterprise environment, port-based security can be enabled on a switch to allow only one MAC address per switch port.

Understand Ethereal Capture and Display Filters

Ethereal is a freeware sniffer that can capture packets from a wired or wireless LAN connection. Here are some examples of Ethereal filters:

- `ip.dst eq www.eccouncil.org`—This sets the filter to capture only packets destined for the webserver `www.eccouncil.org`

- `ip.src == 192.168.1.1`—This sets the filter to capture only packets coming from the host `192.168.1.1`

- `eth.dst eq ff:ff:ff:ff:ff:ff` —This sets the filter to capture only Layer 2 broadcast packets

Practice writing filters in Ethereal that capture only one type of protocol traffic or traffic from a specific source IP or MAC address. It's important to understand how to create these filters before you attempt the CEH exam.

Understand MAC Flooding

A packet sniffer on a switched network can't capture all traffic as it can on a hub network; instead, it captures either traffic coming from or traffic going to the system. It's necessary to use an additional tool to capture all traffic on a switched network. There are essentially two ways to perform active sniffing and make the switch send traffic to the system running the sniffer: ARP spoofing and flooding.

As mentioned earlier, ARP spoofing involves taking on the MAC address of the network gateway and consequently receiving all traffic intended for the gateway on the sniffer system. A hacker can also *flood* a switch with so much traffic that it stops operating as a switch and instead reverts to acting as a hub, sending all traffic to all ports. This active sniffing attack allows the system with the sniffer to capture all traffic on the network.

Understand DNS Spoofing Techniques

DNS spoofing (or *DNS poisoning*) is a technique that tricks a DNS server into believing it has received authentic information when in reality it hasn't. Once the DNS server has been poisoned, the information is generally cached for a while, spreading the effect of the attack to the users of the server. When a user requests a certain website URL, the address is looked up on a DNS server to find the corresponding IP address. If the DNS server has been compromised, the user is redirected to a website other than the one that was requested, such as a fake website.

To perform a DNS attack, the attacker exploits a flaw in the DNS server software that can make it accept incorrect information. If the server doesn't correctly validate DNS responses to ensure that they come from an authoritative source, the server ends up caching the incorrect entries locally and serving them to users that make subsequent requests.

This technique can be used to replace arbitrary content for a set of victims with content of an attacker's choosing. For example, an attacker poisons the IP address's DNS entries for a target website on a given DNS server, replacing them with the IP address of a server the hacker controls. The hacker then creates fake entries for files on this server with names matching those on the target server. These files may contain malicious content, such as a worm or a virus. A user whose computer has referenced the poisoned DNS server is tricked into thinking the content comes from the target server and unknowingly downloads malicious content.

The types of DNS spoofing techniques are as follows:

- Intranet spoofing—acting as a device on the same internal network

- Internet spoofing—acting as a device on the Internet

- Proxy server DNS poisoning—modifying the DNS entries on a proxy server so the user is redirected to a different host system

- DNS cache poisoning—modifying the DNS entries on any system so the user is redirected to a different host

Hacking Tools

EtherFlood is used to flood an Ethernet switch with traffic to make it revert to a hub. By doing this, a hacker is able to capture all traffic on the network rather than just traffic going to and from their system, as would be the case with a switch.

Dsniff is a collection of Unix-executable tools designed to perform network auditing as well as network penetration. The following tools are contained in dsniff: filesnarf, mailsnarf, msgsnarf, urlsnarf, and webspy. These tools passively monitor a vulnerable shared network (such as a LAN where the sniffer sits behind any exterior firewall) for interesting data (passwords, e-mail, files, and so on).

Sshmitm and webmitm implement active man-in-the-middle attacks against redirected Secure Shell (SSH) and HTTPS sessions.

Arpspoof, dnsspoof, and macof work on the interception of switched network traffic that is usually unavailable to a sniffer program because of switching. To get around the layer 2 packet-switching issue, dsniff spoofs the network into thinking that it's a gateway that data must pass through to get outside the network.

IP Restrictions Scanner (IRS) is used to find the IP restrictions that have been set for a particular service on a host. It combines ARP poisoning with a TCP stealth or half-scan technique and exhaustively tests all possible spoofed TCP connections to the selected port of the target. IRS can find servers and network devices like routers and switches and identify access-control features like access control lists (ACLs), IP filters, and firewall rules.

sTerm is a Telnet client with a unique feature: It can establish a bidirectional Telnet session to a target host, without ever sending the real IP and MAC addresses in any packet. Using ARP poisoning, MAC spoofing, and IP spoofing techniques, sTerm can effectively bypass ACLs, firewall rules, and IP restrictions on servers and network devices.

Cain & Abel is a multipurpose hacking tool for Windows. It allows easy recovery of various kinds of passwords by sniffing the network; cracking encrypted passwords using dictionary, brute-force; recording VoIP conversations; decoding scrambled passwords; revealing password boxes; uncovering cached passwords; and analyzing routing protocols. The latest version contains a lot of new features like ARP Poison Routing (APR), which enables sniffing on switched LANs and man-in-the-middle attacks. The sniffer in this version can also analyze encrypted protocols such as SSH-1 and HTTPS, and it contains filters to capture credentials from a wide range of authentication mechanisms.

Packet Crafter is a tool used to create custom TCP/IP/UDP packets. The tool can change the source address of a packet to do IP spoofing and can control IP flags such as checksums and TCP flags such as the state flags, sequence numbers, and ack number.

SMAC is a tool to change the MAC address of a system. It lets a hacker spoof a MAC address when performing an attack.

MAC Changer is a tool used to spoof a MAC address on Unix. It can be used to set the network interface to a specific MAC address, set the MAC randomly, set a MAC of another vendor, set another MAC of the same vendor, set a MAC of the same kind, or even to display a vendor MAC list to choose from.

WinDNSSpoof is a simple DNS ID spoofing tool for Windows. To use it on a switched network, you must be able to sniff traffic of the computer being attacked. Therefore it may need to be used in conjunction with an ARP spoofing or flooding tool.

Distributed DNS Flooder sends a large number of queries to create a DOS attack, disabling DNS. If DNS daemon software logs incorrect queries, the impact of this attack is amplified.

Describe Sniffing Countermeasures

The best security defense against a sniffer on the network is encryption. Although encryption won't prevent sniffing, it renders any data captured during the sniffing attack useless because hacker can't interpret the information. Encryption such as AES and RC4 or RC5 can be utilized in VPN technologies and is a common method to prevent sniffing on a network.

Countermeasures

netINTERCEPTOR is a spam and virus firewall. It has advanced filtering options and can learn and adapt as it identifies new spam. It also intercepts and quarantines the latest e-mail viruses and Trojans, preventing a Trojan from being installed and possibly installing a sniffer.

Sniffdet is a set of tests for remote sniffer detection in TCP/IP network environments. Sniffdet implements various tests for the detection of machines running in promiscuous mode or with a sniffer.

WinTCPKill is a TCP connection termination tool for Windows. The tool requires the ability to use a sniffer to sniff incoming and outgoing traffic of the target. In a switched network, WinTCPKill can use an ARP cache-poisoning tool that performs ARP spoofing.

Exam Essentials

Understand how a sniffer works.   A sniffer operates in promiscuous mode, meaning it captures all traffic regardless of the destination MAC specified in the frame.

Understand the differences between sniffing in a shared network connected via hubs and a switched network.   All traffic is broadcast by a hub, but it's segmented by a switch. To sniff on a switched network, either flooding or ARP spoofing tools must be used.

Know the difference between packets and frames.   Packets are created at layer 3 of the OSI model, and frames are created at layer 2.

Understand how the Address Resolution Protocol works.   ARP is used to find a MAC address from a known IP address by broadcasting the request on the network.

Know the difference between active and passive sniffing.   Active sniffing is used to trick the switch into acting like a hub so that it forwards traffic to the attacker. Passive sniffing captures packets that are already being broadcast on a shared network.

Review Questions

1. What is sniffing?
    A. Sending corrupted data on the network to trick a system
    B. Capturing and deciphering traffic on a network
    C. Corrupting the ARP cache on a target system
    D. Performing a password-cracking attack

2. What is a countermeasure to passive sniffing?
    A. Implementing a switched network
    B. Implementing a shared network
    C. ARP spoofing
    D. Port-based security

3. What type of device connects systems on a shared network?
    A. Routers
    B. Gateways
    C. Hubs
    D. Switches

4. Which of the following is a countermeasure to ARP spoofing?
    A. Port-based security
    B. WinTCPkill
    C. Ethereal
    D. MAC-based security

5. What is dsniff?
    A. A MAC spoofing tool
    B. An IP address spoofing tool
    C. A collection of hacking tools
    D. A sniffer

6. At what layer of the OSI model is data formatted into packets?
    A. Layer 1
    B. Layer 2
    C. Layer 3
    D. Layer 4

7. What is snort?

   A. An IDS and packet sniffer

   B. Only an IDS

   C. Only a packet sniffer

   D. Only a frame sniffer

8. What mode must a network card operate in to perform sniffing?

   A. Shared

   B. Unencrypted

   C. Open

   D. Promiscuous

9. The best defense against any type of sniffing is _____.

   A. Encryption

   B. A switched network

   C. Port-based security

   D. A good security training program

10. For what type of traffic can winsniffer capture passwords? (Choose all that apply.)

   A. POP3

   B. SMTP

   C. HTTP

   D. HTTPS

Answers to Review Questions

1. B. Sniffing is the process of capturing and analyzing data on a network.

2. A. By implementing a switched network, passive sniffing attacks are prevented.

3. C. A network connected via hubs is called a shared network.

4. A. Port-based security implemented on a switch prevents ARP spoofing.

5. C. Dsniff is a group of hacking tools.

6. C. Packets are created and used to carry data at layer 3.

7. A. Snort is both an intrusion detection system (IDS) and a sniffer.

8. D. A network card must operate in promiscuous mode in order to capture traffic destined to a different MAC address than its own.

9. A. Encryption renders the information captured in a sniffer useless to a hacker.

10. A, B, C. Winsniffer can capture passwords for POP3, SMTP, and HTTP traffic.

Chapter

7

Denial of Service and Session Hijacking

CEH EXAM OBJECTIVES COVERED IN THIS CHAPTER:

✓ **Denial of Service**

  ▪ Understand the Types of DoS Attacks

  ▪ Understand How DDoS Attacks Work

  ▪ Understand How BOTs/BOTNETS Work

  ▪ What Is a "Smurf" Attack?

  ▪ What Is "SYN" Flooding?

  ▪ Describe the DoS/DDoS Countermeasures

✓ **Session Hijacking**

  ▪ Understand Spoofing vs. Hijacking

  ▪ List the Types of Session Hijacking

  ▪ Understand Sequence Prediction

  ▪ What Are the Steps in Performing Session Hijacking?

  ▪ Describe How You Would Prevent Session Hijacking

During a Denial of Service (DoS) attack, a hacker renders a system unusable or significantly slows the system by overloading resources or preventing legitimate users from accessing the system. These attacks can be perpetrated against an individual system or an entire network and are usually successful in their attempts.

Session hijacking is a hacking method that creates a temporary DoS for an end user when an attacker takes over the session. Session Hijacking is used by hackers to take over a current session after the user has established an authenticated session. Session hijacking can also be used to perpetrate a man-in-the-middle attack when the hacker steps between the server and legitimate client and intercepts all traffic.

This chapter explains DoS attacks, Distributed Denial of Service (DDoS) attacks, and the elements of session hijacking, such as spoofing methods, the TCP three-way handshake, sequence number prediction, and how hackers use tools for session hijacking. In addition, the countermeasures for DoS and session hijacking are discussed at the end of this chapter.

Denial of Service

A DoS attack is an attempt by a hacker to flood a user's or an organization's system. As a CEH, you need to be familiar with the types of DoS attacks and to understand how DoS and DDoS attacks work. You should also be familiar with robots (BOTs) and robot networks (BOTNETs), as well as smurf attacks and SYN flooding. Finally, as a CEH, you need to be familiar with various DoS and DDoS countermeasures.

Understand the Types of DoS Attacks

There are two main categories of DoS attacks. DoS attacks can be either sent by a single system to a single target (simple DoS) or sent by many systems to a single target (DDoS).

The goal of DoS isn't to gain unauthorized access to machines or data, but to prevent legitimate users of a service from using it. A DoS attack may do the following:

- Flood a network with traffic, thereby preventing legitimate network traffic.

- Disrupt connections between two machines, thereby preventing access to a service.

- Prevent a particular individual from accessing a service.

- Disrupt service to a specific system or person.

Different tools use different types of traffic to flood a victim, but the result is the same: A service on the system or the entire system is unavailable to a user because it's kept busy trying to respond to an exorbitant number of requests.

A DoS attack is usually an attack of last resort. It's considered an unsophisticated attack because it doesn't gain the hacker access to any information but rather annoys the target and interrupts their service. DoS attacks can be destructive and have a substantial impact when sent from multiple systems at the same time (DDoS attacks).

Hacking Tools

Ping of Death is an attack that can cause a system to lock up by sending multiple IP packets, which will be too large for the receiving system when reassembled. Ping of Death can cause a DoS to clients trying to access the server that has been a victim of the attack.

SSPing is a program that sends several large fragmented, Internet Control Message Protocol (ICMP) data packets to a target system. This will cause the computer receiving the data packets to freeze when it tries to reassemble the fragments.

A LAND attack sends a packet to a system where the source IP is set to match the target system's IP address. As a result, the system attempts to reply to itself, causing the system to create a loop which will tie up system resources and eventually may crash the OS.

CPU Hog is a DoS attack tool that uses up the CPU resources on a target system, making it unavailable to the user.

WinNuke is a program that looks for a target system with port 139 open, and sends junk IP traffic to the system on that port. This attack is also known as an Out of Bounds (OOB) attack and causes the IP stack to become overloaded, and eventually the system crashes.

Jolt2 is DoS tool that sends a large number of fragmented IP packets to a Windows target. This ties up system resources and eventually will lock up the system; Jolt2 isn't Windows specific as many Cisco routers and other gateways may be vulnerable to the Jolt2 attack.

Bubonic is a DoS tool which works by sending TCP packets with random settings, in order to increase the load of the target machine so it eventually crashes.

Targa is a program that can be used to run eight different DoS attacks. The attacker has the option to either launch individual attacks or try all of the attacks until one is successful.

RPC Locator is a service that, if unpatched, has a vulnerability to bugger overflows. The RPC Locator service in Windows allows distributed applications to run on the network. It is susceptible to DoS attacks, and many of the tools that perform DoS attacks exploit this vulnerability.

DDoS attacks can be perpetrated by BOTs and BOTNETS, which are compromised systems that an attacker uses to launch the attack against the end victim. The system or network that has been compromised is a secondary victim, whereas the DoS and DDoS attacks flood the primary victim or target.

Understand How DDoS Attacks Work

DDoS is an advanced version of the DoS attack. Like DoS, DDoS also tries to deny access to services running on a system by sending packets to the destination system in a way that the destination system can't handle. The key of a DDoS attack is that it relays attacks from many different hosts (which must first be compromised), rather then from a single host like DoS. DDoS is a large-scale, coordinated attack on a victim system.

Hacking Tools

Trinoo is a tool which sends User Datagram Protocol (UDP) traffic to create a DDoS attack. The Trinoo master is a system used to launch a DoS attack against one or more target systems. The master instructs agent processes (called daemons) on previously compromised systems (secondary victims), to attack one or more IP addresses. This attack occurs for a specified period of time. The Trinoo agent or daemon is installed on a system that suffers from a buffer overflow vulnerability. WinTrinoo is a Windows version of Trinoo and has the same functionality as Trinoo.

Shaft is a derivative of the Trinoo tool that uses UDP communication between masters and agents. Shaft provides statistics on the flood attack that attackers can use to know when the victim system is shut down; Shaft provides UDP, ICMP, and TCP flooding attack options.

Tribal Flood Network (TFN) allows an attacker to use both bandwidth-depletion and resource-depletion attacks. TFN does UDP and ICMP flooding as well as TCP SYN and smurf attacks. TFN2K is based on TFN, with features designed specifically to make TFN2K traffic difficult to recognize and filter. It remotely executes commands, hides the source of the attack using IP address spoofing, and uses multiple transport protocols including UDP, TCP, and ICMP.

Stacheldraht is similar to TFN and includes ICMP flood, UDP flood, and TCP SYN attack options. It also provides a secure Telnet connection (using symmetric key encryption) between the attacker and the agent systems (secondary victims). This prevents system administrators from intercepting and identifying this traffic.

Mstream uses spoofed TCP packets with the ACK flag set to attack a target. It consists of a handler and an agent portion, but access to the handler is password protected.

The services under attack are those of the primary victim; the compromised systems used to launch the attack are secondary victims. These compromised systems, which send the DDoS to the primary victim, are sometimes called *zombies* or *BOTs*. They're usually compromised through another attack and then used to launch an attack on the primary victim at a certain time or under certain conditions. It can be difficult to track the source of the attacks because they originate from several IP addresses.

Normally, DDoS consists of three parts:

- Master/Handler
- Slave/secondary victim/zombie/agent/BOT/BOTNET
- Victim /primary victim

The *master* is the attack launcher. A *slave* is a host that is compromised by and controlled by the master. The *victim* is the target system. The master directs the slaves to launch the attack on the victim system.

DDoS is done in two phases. In the *intrusion phase*, the hacker compromises weak systems in different networks around the world and installs DDoS tools on those compromised slave systems. In the *DDoS attack* phase, the slave systems are triggered to cause them to attack the primary victim.

Understand How BOTs/BOTNETs Work

A BOT is short for web robot and is an automated software program that behaves intelligently. Spammers often use BOTs to automate the posting of spam messages on newsgroups or the sending of emails. BOTs can also be used as remote attack tools. Most often, BOTs are web software agents that interface with web pages. For example, web crawlers (spiders) are web robots that gather web-page information.

The most dangerous BOTs are those that covertly install themselves on users' computers for malicious purposes.

Some BOTs communicate with other users of Internet-based services via instant messaging, Internet Relay Chat (IRC) or another web interface. These BOTs allow IRQ users to ask questions in plain English and then formulate a proper response. Such BOTs can often handle many tasks, including reporting weather, providing zip-code information, listing sports scores, converting units of measure, such as currency, and so on.

A BOTNET is a group of BOT systems. BOTNETs serve various purposes, including DDoS attacks, creation or misuse of Simple Mail Transfer Protocol (SMTP) mail relays for spam, Internet Marketing fraud, the theft of application serial numbers, login IDs, and financial information such as credit card numbers. Generally a BOTNET refers to a group of compromised systems running a BOT for the purpose of launching a coordinated DDOS attack.

What Is a "Smurf" Attack?

A smurf attack sends a large amount of ICMP echo (ping) traffic to a broadcast IP address with the spoofed source address of a victim. Each secondary victim's host on that IP network replies to the ICMP echo request with an echo reply, multiplying the traffic by the number of hosts responding. On a multiaccess broadcast network, hundreds of machines might reply to each packet. This creates a magnified DoS attack of ping replies, flooding the primary victim. IRC servers are the primary victim of smurf attacks on the Internet.

What Is "SYN" Flooding?

A SYN flood attack sends TCP connection requests faster than a machine can process them. The attacker creates a random source address for each packet and sets the SYN flag to request a new connection to the server from the spoofed IP address. The victim responds to the spoofed IP address and then waits for the TCP confirmation that never arrives. Consequently, the victim's connection table fills up waiting for replies; after the table is full, all new connections are ignored. Legitimate users are ignored, as well, and can't access the server. Some of the methods to prevent SYN Flood attacks are SYN cookies, RST cookies, Micro Blocks, and Stack Tweaking.

Describe the DoS/DDoS Countermeasures

There are several ways to detect, halt, or prevent DoS attacks. The following are common security features available:

Network-ingress filtering   All network access providers should implement network-ingress filtering to stop any downstream networks from injecting packets with faked or spoofed addresses into the Internet. Although this doesn't stop an attack from occurring, it does make it much easier to track down the source of the attack and terminate the attack quickly.

Rate-limiting network traffic   A number of routers in the market today have features that let you limit the amount of bandwidth some types of traffic can consume. This is sometimes referred to as *traffic shaping*.

Intrusion detection systems   Use an intrusion detection system (IDS) to detect attackers who are communicating with slave, master, or agent machines. Doing so lets you know whether a machine in your network is being used to launch a known attack but probably won't detect new variations of these attacks or the tools that implement them. Most IDS vendors have signatures to detect Trinoo, TFN, or Stacheldraht network traffic.

Host-auditing tools   File-scanning tools are available that attempt to detect the existence of known DDoS tool client and server binaries in a system.

Network-auditing tools   Network-scanning tools are available that attempt to detect the presence of DDoS agents running on hosts on your network.

Automated network-tracing tools   Tracing streams of packets with spoofed address through the network is a time-consuming task that requires the cooperation of all networks carrying the traffic and that must be completed while the attack is in progress.

DoS Scanning Tools

Find_ddos is a tool that scans a local system that likely contains a DDoS program. It can detect several known DoS attack tools.

SARA gathers information about remote hosts and networks by examining network services. This includes information about the network information services as well as potential security flaws such as incorrectly set up or configured network services, well-known bugs in the system or network utilities system software vulnerabilities listed in the Common Vulnerabilities and Exposures (CVE) database, and weak policy decisions.

RID is a free scanning tool that detects the presence of Trinoo, TFN, or Stacheldraht clients.

Zombie Zapper instructs zombie routines to go to sleep, thus stopping their attack. You can use the same commands an attacker would use to stop the attack.

Session Hijacking

Session hijacking is when a hacker takes control of a user session after the user has successfully authenticated with a server. Session hijacking involves an attack identifying the current session IDs of a client/server communication and taking over the client's session. Session hijacking is made possible by tools that perform sequence-number prediction. The details of sequence-number prediction will be discussed later in this chapter.

Understand Spoofing vs. Hijacking

Spoofing attacks are different from hijacking attacks. In a spoofing attack, the hacker performs sniffing and listens to traffic as it's passed along the network from sender to receiver. The hacker then uses the information gathered to spoof or uses an address of a legitimate system. Hijacking involves actively taking another user offline to perform the attack. The attacker relies on the legitimate user to make a connection and authenticate. After that, the attacker takes over the session, and the valid user's session is disconnected.

Session hijacking involves the following three steps to perpetuate an attack:

Tracking the session   The hacker identifies an open session and predicts the sequence number of the next packet.

Desynchronizing the connection   The hacker sends the valid user's system a TCP reset (RST) or finish (FIN) packet to cause them to close their session.

Injecting the attacker's packet   The hacker sends the server a TCP packet with the predicted sequence number, and the server accepts it as the valid user's next packet.

List the Types of Session Hijacking

Hackers can use two types of session hijacking: active and passive. The primary difference between active and passive hijacking is the hacker's level of involvement in the session. In an active attack, an attacker finds an active session and takes over the session by using tools that predict the next sequence number used in the TCP session.

In a passive attack, an attacker hijacks a session and then watches and records all the traffic that is being sent by the legitimate user. Passive session hijacking is really no more than sniffing. It's used to gather information such as passwords and then to use that information later to authenticate as a separate session.

TCP Concepts: Three-Way Handshake

One of the key features of TCP is reliability and ordered delivery of packets. To accomplish this, TCP uses acknowledgment (ACK) packets and sequence numbers. Manipulating these numbers is the basis for TCP session hijacking. To understand session hijacking, let's review the TCP three-way handshake described in earlier chapters:

1. The valid user initiates a connection with the server. This is accomplished by the valid user sending a packet to the server with the SYN bit set and the user's initial Sequence Number (ISN).

2. The server receives this packet and sends back a packet with the SYN bit set and an ISBN for the server, plus the ACK bit set identifying the user's ISN incremented by a value of one.

3. The valid user acknowledges the server by returning a packet with the ACK bit set and incrementing the servers ISN by one.

This connection can be closed from either side due to a timeout, or upon receipt of a package with the FIN or RST flag set.

Upon receipt of a packet with the RST flag set, the receiving system closes the connection, and any incoming packets for the session are discarded. If the FIN flag is set in a packet, then the receiving system goes through the process of closing the connection, and any packets received while closing the connection are still processed. Sending a packet with the FIN or RST flag set is the most common method hijackers use to close the client's session with the server and take over the session by acting as the client.

Understand Sequence Prediction

TCP is a connection-oriented protocol, responsible for reassembling streams of packets into their original intended order. Therefore, each packet must have a unique number known as a sequence number (SN). Every packet has to be assigned a unique session number that enables the receiving machine to reassemble the stream of packets into their original and intended order; this unique number is known as a *sequence number*. If the packets arrive out of order, as happens regularly over the Internet, then the sequence number is used to stream the packets correctly. As just illustrated, the system initiating a TCP session transmits a packet with the SYN bit set. This is called a *synchronize packet* and includes the client's Initial Sequence Number (ISN). The ISN is a pseudo-randomly generated number with over 4 billion possible combinations, yet it is statistically possible for it to repeat.

When the acknowledgment (ACK) packet is sent, each machine uses the SN from the packet being acknowledged, plus an increment. This not only properly confirms receipt of a specific packet, but also tells the sender the next expected TCP packet sequence number. Within the three-way handshake, the increment value is 1. In normal data communications, the increment value equals the size of the data in bytes (for example, if you transmit 45 bytes of data, the ACK responds using the incoming packet's SN plus 45.

Figure 7.1 illustrates the sequence numbers and acknowledgments used during the TCP three-way handshake.

FIGURE 7.1   Sequence numbers and acknowledgment during the TCP three-way handshake

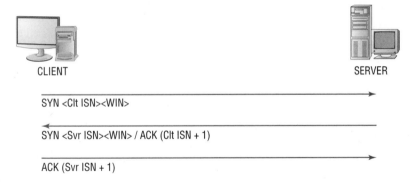

SYN <Clt ISN><WIN>

SYN <Svr ISN><WIN> / ACK (Clt ISN + 1)

ACK (Svr ISN + 1)

Hacking tools used to perform session hijacking do sequence number prediction. In order to successfully perform a TCP sequence prediction attack, the hacker must sniff the traffic between two systems. Next, the hacker or the hacking tool must successfully guess the sequence number or locate an ISN to calculate the next sequence number. This can be more difficult than it sounds, because packets travel very fast.

When the hacker is unable to sniff the connection, it becomes much more difficult to guess the next sequence number. For this reason, most session-hijacking tools include features to permit sniffing the packets to determine the sequence numbers.

Hackers generate packets using a spoofed IP address of the system that had a session with the target system. The hacking tools issue packets with the sequence numbers that the target system is expecting. But the hacker's packets must arrive before the packets from the trusted system whose connection is being hijacked. This is accomplished by flooding the trusted system with packets or sending a RST packet to the trusted system so that it is unavailable to send packets to the target system.

What Are the Steps in Performing Session Hijacking?

In summary, session hijacking involves the following three steps to perpetuate the attack:

Tracking the session   The hacker identifies an open session and predicts the sequence number of the next packet.

Desynchronizing the connection   The hacker sends the valid user's system a TCP reset (RST) or finish (FIN) packet to cause them to close their session. Alternately the hacker can use a DoS tool to disconnect the user from the server.

Injecting the attacker's packet   The hacker sends the server a TCP packet with the predicted sequence number, and the server accepts it as the valid user's next packet.

Hacking Tools

Juggernaut is a network sniffer that can be used to hijack TCP sessions. It runs on Linux operating systems and can be used to watch for all network traffic, or it can be given a keyword such as a password to look for. The program shows all active network connections and the attacker can then choose a session to hijack.

Hunt is a program that can be used to sniff and hijack active sessions on a network. Hunt performs connection management, Address Resolution Protocol (ARP) spoofing, resetting of connections, monitoring of connections, Media Access Control (MAC) address discovery, and sniffing of TCP traffic.

TTYWatcher is a session-hijacking utility that allows the hijiacker to return the stolen session to the valid user as though it was never hijacked. TTYWatcher is only for Sun Solaris systems.

IP Watcher is a commercial session-hijacking tool that lets an attacker monitor connections and take over a session. This program can monitor all connections on a network, allowing the attacker to watch an exact copy of a session in real time.

T-Sight is a session monitoring and hijacking tool for Windows that can assist when an attempt at a network break-in or compromise occurs. With T-Sight, a systems administrator can monitor all network connections in real time and observe any suspicious activity that takes place. T-Sight can also hijack any TCP session on the network. For security reasons, Engarde Systems licenses this software only to predetermined IP addresses.

The Remote TCP Session Reset Utility displays current TCP session and connection information such as IP addresses and port numbers. The utility is primarily used to reset TCP sessions.

Dangers Posed by Session Hijacking

TCP session hijacking is a dangerous attack: Most systems are vulnerable to it, because they use TCP/IP as their primary communication protocol. Newer operating systems have attempted to secure themselves from session hijacking by using pseudorandom number generators to calculate the ISN, making the sequence number harder to guess. However, this security measure is ineffective if the attacker is able to sniff packets, which gives all the information required to perform this attack.

The following are reasons why it's important for a CEH to be aware of session hijacking:

- Most computers are vulnerable.
- Few countermeasures are available to adequately protect against it.
- Session hijacking attacks are simple to launch.
- Hijacking is dangerous because of the information that can be gathered during the attack.

Describe How You Would Prevent Session Hijacking

To defend against session hijack attacks, a network should employ several defenses. The most effective protection is encryption, such as Internet Protocol Security (IPSec). This also defends against any other attack vectors that depend on sniffing. Attackers may be able to passively monitor your connection, but they won't be able to interpret the encrypted data. Other countermeasures include using encrypted applications such as Secure Shell (SSH, an encrypted Telnet) and Secure Sockets Layer (SSL, for HTTPS traffic).

You can help prevent session hijacking by reducing the potential methods of gaining access to your network—for example, by eliminating remote access to internal systems. If the network has remote users who need to connect to carry out their duties, then use virtual private networks (VPNs) that have been secured with tunneling protocols and encryption (Layer 3 Tunneling Protocol [L3TP]/Point-to-Point Tunneling Protocol [PPTP] and IPSec).

The use of multiple safety nets is always the best countermeasure to any potential threat. Employing any one countermeasure may not be enough, but using them together to secure your enterprise will make the attack success rate minimal for anyone but the most professional and dedicated attacker. The following is a checklist of countermeasures that should be employed to prevent session hijacking:

- Use encryption.
- Use a secure protocol.
- Limit incoming connections.
- Minimize remote access.
- Have strong authentication.
- Educate your employees.
- Maintain different username and passwords for different accounts.

Exam Essentials

Know the purpose of a DoS attack.   The purpose of a DoS attack is to send so much traffic to a target system that users are prevented from accessing the system.

Understand the difference between DoS and DDoS.   A Distributed Denial of Service (DDoS) attack is a coordinated attack by many systems sent to one target, whereas DoS involves a single system attacking the target.

Know how to prevent DoS attacks.   Network traffic filtering, IDS, and auditing tools are all ways to detect and prevent DoS attacks.

Know the two phases of DDoS.   During the first phase, systems are compromised and DDoS tools are installed, making the systems zombies or slaves; this is called the intrusion phase. The second phase involves launching an attack against the victim system.

Know what a zombie or slave is in a DDoS attack.   A zombie or slave is a system that has been compromised by a hacker and can be commanded to participate in the sending of a DDoS attack to a target system.

Know what a master is in a DDoS attack.   The master is the controlling system in a DDoS attack scenario. It tells the zombies when to launch the attack.

Understand session hijacking and how it occurs.   Session hijacking involves taking over another user's session after they have authenticated in order to gain access to a system.

Understand the difference between spoofing and hijacking.   Spoofing involves artificial identification of a packets' source address, where that address is often deduced from sniffed network traffic, where hijacking refers to a compromised session—normally one in which the attacker takes the user offline and uses their session.

Understand the difference between active and passive session hijacking.   Active session hijacking is the more common of the two types and involves taking over another user's session and desynchronizing the valid user's connection. Passive hijacking monitors the session and allows a hacker to gather confidential information via sniffing packets.

Be familiar with some of the tools used to perform session hijacking.   Juggernaut, Hunt, TTYWatcher, IP watcher, T-Sight, TCP reset utility are all session hijacking tools.

Understand the importance of sequence numbers in a session hijacking attack.   It's necessary to either guess or locate sequence numbers in order to initiate a session hijacking attack. Sequence numbers are used to sequentialize packets and permit a receiving station to reassemble data correctly.

Understand the dangers of session hijacking.   Most computers are vulnerable to session hijacking attacks, and available countermeasures aren't always successful. Confidential and important information, such as passwords, account information, and credit card numbers can be obtained through session-hijacking attacks.

Know the countermeasures to session hijacking.   Use encryption, strong authentication, and secure protocols; limit incoming connections, minimize remote access connections, educate employees, and maintain unique usernames and passwords for different accounts.

Review Questions

1. Which is a method to prevent Denial of Service attacks?

   A. Static routing

   B. Traffic filtering

   C. Firewall rules

   D. Personal firewall

2. What is a zombie?

   A. A compromised system used to launch a DDoS attack

   B. The hacker's computer

   C. The victim of a DDoS attack

   D. A compromised system that is the target of a DDoS attack

3. The Trinoo tool uses what protocol to perform a DoS attack?

   A. TCP

   B. IP

   C. UDP

   D. HTTP

4. What is the first phase of a DDoS attack?

   A. Intrusion

   B. Attack

   C. DoS

   D. Finding a target system

5. Which tool can run eight different types of DoS attacks?

   A. Ping of Death

   B. Trinoo

   C. Targa

   D. TFN2K

6. What is a smurf attack?

   A. Sending a large amount of ICMP traffic with a spoofed source address

   B. Sending a large amount of TCP traffic with a spoofed source address

   C. Sending a large number of TCP connection requests with a spoofed source address

   D. Sending a large number of TCP connection requests

7. What is a LAND attack?

   A. Sending oversized ICMP packets

   B. Sending packets to a victim with a source address set to the victim's IP address

   C. Sending packets to a victim with a destination address set to the victim's IP address

   D. Sending a packet with the same source and destination address

8. What is the Ping of Death?

   A. Sending packets that, when reassembled, are too large for the system to understand

   B. Sending very large packets that cause a buffer overflow

   C. Sending packets very quickly to fill up the receiving buffer

   D. Sending TCP packet with the fragment offset out of bounds

9. How does a Denial of Service attack work?

   A. Cracks passwords, causing the system to crash

   B. Imitates a valid user

   C. Prevents a legitimate user from using a system or service

   D. Attempts to break the authentication method

10. What is the goal of a Denial of Service attack?

   A. Capture files from a remote system

   B. Incapacitate a system or network

   C. Exploit a weakness in the TCP/IP stack

   D. Execute a Trojan using the hidden shares

11. Which of the following tools is only for Sun Solaris systems?

   A. Juggernaut

   B. T-Sight

   C. IP Watcher

   D. TTYWatcher

12. What is a sequence number?

   A. A number that indicates where a packet falls in the data stream

   B. A way of sending information from the sending to the receiving station

   C. A number that the hacker randomly chooses in order to hijack a session

   D. A number used in reconstructing UDP session

13. What type of information can be obtained during a session-hijacking attack? (Choose all that apply.)

   A. Passwords

   B. Credit card numbers

   C. Confidential data

   D. Authentication information

14. Which of the following is essential information to a hacker performing a session-hijacking attack?

   A. Session ID

   B. Session number

   C. Sequence number

   D. Source IP address

15. Which of the following is a session-hijacking tool that runs on Linux operating systems?

   A. Juggernaut

   B. Hunt

   C. TTYWatcher

   D. TCP Reset Utility

16. Which of the following is the best countermeasure to session hijacking?

   A. Port filtering firewall

   B. Encryption

   C. Session monitoring

   D. Strong passwords

17. Which of the following best describes sniffing?

   A. Gathering packets to locate IP addresses, in order to initiate a session-hijacking attack

   B. Analyzing packets in order to locate the sequence number to start a session hijack

   C. Monitoring TCP sessions in order to initiate a session-hijacking attack

   D. Locating a host susceptible to a session-hijack attack

18. What is session hijacking?

   A. Monitoring UDP session

   B. Monitoring TCP sessions

   C. Taking over UDP sessions

   D. Taking over TCP sessions

19. What types of packets are sent to the victim of a session-hijacking attack to cause them to close their end of the connection?

   A. FIN and ACK

   B. SYN or ACK

   C. SYN and ACK

   D. FIN or RST

20. What is an ISN?

   A. Initiation Session Number

   B. Initial Sequence Number

   C. Initial Session Number

   D. Indication Sequence Number

Answers to Review Questions

1. B. Traffic filtering is a method to prevent DoS attacks.

2. A. A zombie is a compromised system used to launch a DDoS attack.

3. C. Trinoo uses UDP to flood the target system with data.

4. A. The intrusion phase compromises and recruits zombie systems to use in the coordinated attack phase.

5. C. Targa is able to send eight different types of DoS attacks.

6. A. A smurf attack sends a large number of ICMP request frames with a spoofed address of the victim system.

7. B. A LAND attack sends packets to a system with that system as the source address, causing the system to try to reply to itself.

8. A. The Ping of Death attack sends packets that, when reassembled, are too large and cause the system to crash or lock up.

9. C. A Denial of Service attack works by preventing legitimate users from accessing the system.

10. B. The goal of a Denial of Service attack is to overload a system and cause it to stop responding.

11. D. TTYWatcher is used to perform session hijacking on Sun Solaris systems.

12. A. A sequence number indicates where the packet is located in the data steam so the receiving station can reassemble the data.

13. A, B, C. Passwords, credit card numbers, and other confidential data can be gathered in a session-hijacking attack. Authentication information isn't accessible because session hijacking occurs after the user has authenticated.

14. C. In order to perform a session-hijacking attack, the hacker must know the sequence number to use in the next packet so the server will accept the packet.

15. A. Juggernaut runs on Linux operating systems.

16. B. Encryption make any information the hacker gathers during a session-hijacking attempt unreadable.

17. B. Sniffing is usually used to locate the sequence number, which is necessary for a session hijack.

18. D. The most common form of session hijacking is the process of taking over a TCP session.

19. D. FIN (finish) and RST (reset) packets are sent to the victim to desynchronize their connection and cause them to close the existing connection.

20. B. ISN is the Initial Sequence Number that is sent by the host and is the starting point for the sequence numbers used in later packets.

Chapter

8

Hacking Web Servers, Web Application Vulnerabilities, and Web-Based Password Cracking Techniques

---

CEH EXAM OBJECTIVES COVERED IN THIS CHAPTER:

✓ **Hacking Web Servers**

- List the Types of Web Server Vulnerabilities
- Understand the Attacks against Web Servers
- Understand IIS Unicode Exploits
- Understand Patch Management Techniques
- Understand Web Application Scanner
- What Is Metasploit Framework?
- Describe Web Server Hardening Methods

✓ **Web Application Vulnerabilities**

- Understanding How Web Applications Work
- Objectives of Web Application Hacking
- Anatomy of an Attack
- Web Application Threats
- Understand Google Hacking
- Understand Web Application Countermeasures

✓ **Web-Based Password Cracking Techniques**

- List the Authentication Types
- What Is a Password Cracker?
- How Does a Password Cracker Work?
- Understand Password Attacks—Classification
- Understand Password Cracking Countermeasures

Web servers and web applications have a very high potential to be compromised. The primary reason for this is that the systems that run web server software must be publicly available on the Internet. Once a web server has been compromised, the system can provide hackers another door into the network. Not only the web server software, but also applications that run on the web server, are open to attack and can be exploited. Due to their function, web servers are more accessible than other systems and less protected, so they're easier to exploit.

A web server is available via the Internet 24/7, which makes it a fairly easy attack point on the network. This chapter will discuss types of attacks performed against web servers, as well as web applications and their vulnerabilities.

Hacking Web Servers

As a Certified Ethical Hacker, understanding how web servers are hacked is an important part of your job. This includes knowing their vulnerabilities, as well as understanding the types of attacks—including Internet Information Server (IIS) Unicode exploits—a hacker may use. In addition, you should know when to use patch-management techniques and understand the methods used to harden web servers.

We'll look at all these topics in the following sections.

List the Types of Web Server Vulnerabilities

Web servers, like other systems, can be compromised by a hacker. The following vulnerabilities are most commonly exploited in web servers:

- Misconfiguration of the web server software

- Operating system or application bugs, or flaws in programming code

- Vulnerable default installation of operating system and web server software, and/or lack of patch management to update operating system or web server software

- Lack of or not following proper security policies and procedures

Hackers exploit these vulnerabilities to gain access to the web server. Because web servers are located in a Demilitarized Zone (DMZ), which is a publicly accessible area between two packet filtering devices, and can be more easily accessed by the organization's client systems, an exploit of a web server offers a hacker easier access to internal systems or databases.

Website Cloaking is the ability of a web server to display different types of web pages based on the user's IP address.

Understand the Attacks against Web Servers

The most visible type of attack against web servers is defacement. Hackers deface websites for sheer joy and an opportunity to enhance their reputations. *Defacing* a website means the hacker exploits a vulnerability in the operating system or web server software and then alters the website files to show that the site has been hacked. Often the hacker displays their hacker name on the website's home page.

Common website attacks that enable a hacker to deface a website include the following:

- Capturing administrator credentials through man-in-the-middle attacks
- Revealing an administrator password through a brute-force attack
- Using a DNS attack to redirect users to a different web server
- Compromising an FTP or e-mail server
- Exploiting web application bugs that result in a vulnerability
- Misconfiguring web shares
- Taking advantages of weak permissions
- Rerouting a client after a firewall or router attack
- Using SQL injection attacks (if the SQL server and web server are the same system)
- Using Telnet or Secure Shell (SSH) intrusion
- Carrying out URL poisoning, which redirects the user to a different URL
- Using web server extension or remote service intrusion
- For cookie-enabled security—Intercept the communication between the client and the server and change the cookie to make the server believe that there is a user with higher privileges

Understand IIS Unicode Exploits

Windows 2000 systems running IIS are susceptible to a directory traversal attack, also known as the Unicode exploit. The vulnerability in IIS, which allows for the directory traversal/Unicode exploit, occurs only in unpatched Windows 2000 systems and affects CGI scripts and ISAPI extensions such as .ASP. The vulnerability exists because the IIS parser was not properly interpreting unicode, allowing hackers system level access.

Essentially, Unicode converts characters of any language to a universal hex code specification. However, the unicode is interpreted twice, and the parser only scanned the resultant request once (following the first interpretation). Hackers could therefore sneak file requests through IIS. For example, utilizing %c0% af instead of a slash in a relative pathname exploits the IIS vulnerability.

In some cases, the request lets the hacker gain access to files that they otherwise shouldn't be able to see. The Unicode directory traversal vulnerability allows a hacker to add, change, or delete files, or upload and run code on the server. The ability to add or run files on the system allows a hacker to install a Trojan or backdoor on the system.

The IIS Unicode exploit is an outdated vulnerability and is presented in this text as a proof of concept—that is, proof that the vulnerability exists and can be exploited.

Understand Patch Management Techniques

Patch management is the process of updating appropriate patches and hotfixes required by a system vendor. Proper patch management involves choosing how patches are to be installed and verified, and testing those patches on a nonproduction network prior to installation.

You should maintain a log of all patches applied to each system. To make patch installation easier, you can use automated patch-management systems provided by PatchLink, St. Bernard, Microsoft, and other software vendors to assess your systems and decide which patches to deploy.

Hacking Tools

N-Stalker Web Application Security Scanner allows you to assess a web application for a large number of vulnerabilities including cross-site scripting, SQL injection, buffer overflow, and parameter-tampering attacks.

The Metasploit framework is a freeware tool used to test or hack operating systems or web server software. Exploits can be used as plug-ins, and testing can be performed from a Windows or Unix platform. Metasploit was originally a command-line utility, but it now has a web browser interface. Using Metasploit, hackers can write their own exploits as well as utilizing standard exploits.

CORE IMPACT and SAINT Vulnerability Scanner are commercial exploit tools used to test and compromise operating systems and web server software.

Describe Web Server Hardening Methods

A web server administrator can do many things to *harden* a server (increase its security). The following are ways to increase the security of the web server:

- Rename the administrator account, and use a strong password.
- Disable default websites and FTP sites.
- Remove unused applications from the server, such as WebDAV.

- Disable directory browsing in the web server's configuration settings.

- Add a legal notice to the site to make potential attackers aware of the implications of hacking the site.

- Apply the most current patches, hotfixes, and service packs to the operating system and web server software.

- Perform bounds-checking on input for web forms and query strings to prevent buffer overflow or malicious input attacks.

- Disable remote administration.

- Use a script to map unused file extensions to a 404 ("File not found") error message.

- Enable auditing and logging.

- Use a firewall between the web server and the Internet and allow only necessary ports (such as 80 and 443) through the firewall.

- Replace the GET with POST method when sending data to a web server

 A countermeasure to cross site scripting is to replace "<" and ">" characters with "<" and ">" using server scripts. A countermeasure to SSL attacks is to install a proxy server and terminate SSL at the proxy or install a hardware SSL accelerator and terminate SSL at this layer.

Web Application Vulnerabilities

In addition to understanding how a hacker can exploit a web server, it's also important for a CEH to be familiar with web application vulnerabilities. In this section, we'll discuss how web applications work, as well as the objectives of web application hacking. We'll also examine the anatomy of a web application attack and some actual web application threats. Finally, we'll look at Google hacking and countermeasures you should be familiar with.

Understanding How Web Applications Work

Web applications are programs that reside on a web server to give the user functionality beyond just a website. Database queries, webmail, discussion groups, and blogs are all examples of web applications.

A web application uses a client/server architecture, with a web browser as the client and the web server acting as the application server. JavaScript is a popular way to implement web applications. Since web applications are widely implemented, any user with a web browser can interact with most site utilities.

Objectives of Web Application Hacking

The purpose of hacking a web application is to gain confidential data. Web applications are critical to the security of a system because they usually connect to a database that contains information such as identities with credit card numbers and passwords. Web application vulnerabilities increase the threat that hackers will exploit the operating system and web server or web application software. Web applications are essentially another door into a system and can be exploited to compromise the system.

Anatomy of an Attack

Hacking web applications is similar to hacking other systems. Hackers follow a five-step process: They scan a network, gather information to test different attack scenarios, and finally plan and launch an attack. The steps are listed in Figure 8.1.

FIGURE 8.1   The stages of a web application attack

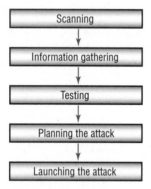

Web Application Threats

Many web application threats exist on a web server. The following are the most common threats:

Cross-site scripting   A parameter entered into a web form is processed by the web application. The correct combination of variables can result in arbitrary command execution.

SQL injection   Inserting SQL commands into the URL gets the database server to dump, alter, delete, or create information in the database.

Command injection   The hacker inserts programming commands into a web form.

Cookie poisoning and snooping   The hacker corrupts or steals cookies.

Buffer overflow   Huge amounts of data are sent to a web application through a web form to execute commands.

Authentication hijacking   The hacker steals a session once a user has authenticated.

Directory traversal / Unicode   The hacker browses through the folders on a system via a web browser or Windows explorer.

Hacking Tools

Instant Source allows a hacker to see and edit HTML source code. It can be used directly from within the web browser.

Wget is a command-line tool that a hacker can use to download an entire website, complete with all the files. The hacker can view the source code offline and test certain attacks prior to launching them against the real web server.

WebSleuth uses spidering technology to index an entire website. For example, WebSleuth can pull all the e-mail addresses from different pages of a website.

BlackWidow can scan and map all the pages of a website to create a profile of the site.

SiteScope maps out the connections within a web application and aids in the deconstruction of the program.

WSDigger is a web services testing tool that contains sample attack plug-ins for SQL injection, cross-site scripting, and other web attacks.

Burp is a Windows-based automated attack tool for web applications. It can also be used to guess passwords on web applications and perform man-in-the-middle attacks.

Understand Google Hacking

Google hacking refers to using Google's powerful search engine to locate high-value targets or to search for valuable information such as passwords.

Many tools such as http://johnny.ihackstuff.com and Acunetix Web Vulnerability Scanner contain a list of Google hacking terms organized in a database, to make searching easier. For example, you can enter the term *password* or *medical records* into the Google search engine and see what information is available. Many times, Google can pull information directly out of private databases or documents.

Understand Web Application Countermeasures

Countermeasures exist for common web application vulnerabilities. Following are countermeasures for each of the web application vulnerabilities listed in the previous section:

Cross-site scripting   Validate cookies, query strings, form fields, and hidden fields.

SQL injection   Validate user variables.

Command injection   Use language-specific libraries for the programming language.

Cookie poisoning and snooping   Don't store passwords in a cookie. Implement cookie time-outs, and authenticate cookies.

Buffer overflow   Validate user input length, and perform bounds checking.

Authentication hijacking   Use SSL to encrypt traffic.

Directory traversal / Unicode   Define access rights to private folders on the web server. Apply patches and hotfixes.

Web-Based Password Cracking Techniques

As a CEH, you need to be familiar with the techniques hackers use to crack web-based passwords. This includes being able to list the different authentication types, knowing what a password cracker is, identifying the classifications of password-cracking techniques, and knowing the available countermeasures. We'll look at each in the following sections.

List the Authentication Types

Web servers and web applications support multiple authentication types. The most common is HTTP authentication. There are two types of HTTP authentication: basic and digest. HTTP authentication sends the username and password in cleartext, whereas digest authentication hashes the credentials and uses a challenge-response model for authentication.

In addition, web servers and web applications support NTLM, certificate-based, token-based, and biometric authentication. NTLM authentication uses Internet Explorer and IIS web servers, making NTLM more suitable for internal authentication on an intranet that uses the Microsoft operating systems. Windows 2000 and 2003 servers utilize Kerberos authentication for a more secure option. Certificate-based authentication uses an x.509 certificate for public/private key technology. A *token*, such as SecurID, is a hardware device that displays an authentication code for 60 seconds; a user uses this code to log in to a network. Biometric authentication uses a physical characteristic such as fingerprint, eye iris, or handprint to authenticate the user.

What Is a Password Cracker?

A *password cracker* is a program designed to decrypt passwords or disable password protection. Password crackers rely on dictionary searches (attacks) or brute-force methods to crack passwords.

How Does a Password Cracker Work?

The first step in a dictionary attack is to is to generate a list of potential passwords that can be found in a dictionary. The hacker usually creates this list with a dictionary generator program or dictionaries that can be downloaded from the Internet. Next, the list of dictionary words is hashed or encrypted. This hash list is compared against the hashed password the hacker is trying to crack. The hacker can get the hashed password by sniffing it from a wired or wireless network or directly from the Security Accounts Manager

(SAM) or shadow password files on the hard drive of a system. Finally, the program displays the unencrypted version of the password. Dictionary password crackers can only discover passwords that are dictionary words.

If the user has implemented a strong password, then brute-force password cracking can be implemented. Brute-force password crackers try every possible combination of letters, numbers, and special characters, which takes much longer than a dictionary attack because of the number of permutations.

Understand Password Attacks: Classification

The three types of password attacks are as follows:

Dictionary   Uses passwords that can be found in a dictionary

Brute force   Guesses complex passwords that use letters, numbers, and special characters

Hybrid   Uses dictionary words with a number or special character as a substitute for a letter.

Hacking Tool

Webcracker is a tool that uses a word list to attempt to log on to a web server. It looks for the "HTTP 302 object moved" response to make guesses on the password. From this response the tool can determine the authentication type in use and attempt to log on to the system.

Understand Password-Cracking Countermeasures

The best password-cracking countermeasure is to implement strong passwords that are at least eight characters long (the old standard was six) and that include alphanumeric characters. Usernames and passwords should be different, because many usernames are transmitted in cleartext. Complex passwords that require uppercase, lowercase, and numbers or special characters are harder to crack. You should also implement a strong authentication mechanism such as Kerberos or tokens to protect passwords in transit.

Exam Essentials

Know the types of web server vulnerabilities.   Misconfiguration, operating system or application bugs and flaws, default installation of operating system and web server software, lack of patch management, and lack of proper security policies and procedures are all web server vulnerabilities.

Know common web application threats.   Cross-site scripting, SQL and command injection, cookie poisoning and snooping, buffer overflow, authentication hijacking, and directory traversal are all common web application threats.

Understand Google hacking.   Google hacking involves using the Google search engine to locate passwords, credit card numbers, medical records, or other confidential information.

Understand Patch Management Techniques   Patch management is important for ensuring a system is up to date on the latest security fixes. A process for testing, applying, and logging patches to a system should be defined and followed.

Know the different authentication mechanisms for web servers.   HTTP basic and digest authentication, NTLM, tokens, biometrics certificates are all methods of authenticating to a web server.

Understand how password crackers work.   Password crackers use a hashed dictionary file to crack a password.

Know the types of password attacks.   Dictionary, hybrid, and brute force are the three types of password attacks.

Review Questions

1. Which of the following are types of HTTP web authentication? (Choose all that apply.)

   A. Digest

   B. Basic

   C. Windows

   D. Kerberos

2. Which of the following is a countermeasure for a buffer overflow attack?

   A. Input field length validation

   B. Encryption

   C. Firewall

   D. Use of web forms

3. A hardware device that displays a login that changes every 60 seconds is known as a/an _____.

   A. Login finder

   B. Authentication server

   C. Biometric authentication

   D. Token

4. Which is a common web server vulnerability?

   A. Limited user accounts

   B. Default installation

   C. Open shares

   D. No directory access

5. A password of *P@SSWORD* can be cracked using which type of attack?

   A. Brute force

   B. Hybrid

   C. Dictionary

   D. Zero day exploit

6. Which of the following is a countermeasure for authentication hijacking?

   A. Authentication logging

   B. Kerberos

   C. SSL

   D. Active Directory

7. Why is a web server more commonly attacked than other systems?

   A. Always accessible

   B. Does not require much hacking ability

   C. Difficult to exploit

   D. Simple to exploit

8. A client-server program that resides on a web server is called a/an _____.

   A. Internet program

   B. Web application

   C. Patch

   D. Configuration file

9. Which is a countermeasure to a directory-traversal attack?

   A. Enforce permissions to folders.

   B. Allow everyone access to the default page only.

   C. Allow only registered users to access the home page of a website.

   D. Make all users log in to access folders.

10. What is it called when a hacker inserts programming commands into a web form?

   A. Form tampering

   B. Command injection

   C. Buffer overflow

   D. Web form attack

Answers to Review Questions

1. A, B. Digest and basic are the types of HTTP web authentication.

2. A. Validating the field length and performing bounds checking are countermeasures for a buffer overflow attack.

3. D. A token is a hardware device containing a screen that displays a discrete set of numbers used for login and authentication.

4. B. Default installation is a common web server vulnerability.

5. B. A hybrid attack substitutes numbers and special characters for letters.

6. C. SSL is a countermeasure for authentication hijacking.

7. A. A web server is always accessible, so a hacker can hack it more easily than less-available systems.

8. B. Web applications are client-server programs that reside on a web server.

9. A. A countermeasure to a directory-traversal attack is to enforce permissions to folders.

10. B. Command injection involves a hacker entering programming commands into a web form in order to get the web server to execute the commands.

Chapter

9

SQL Injection and Buffer Overflows

CEH EXAM OBJECTIVES COVERED IN THIS CHAPTER:

✓ **SQL Injection**

- ▪ What Is SQL Injection?
- ▪ Understand the Steps to Conduct SQL Injection
- ▪ Understand SQL Server Vulnerabilities
- ▪ Describe SQL Injection Countermeasures

✓ **Buffer Overflows**

- ▪ Identify the Different Types of Buffer Overflows and Methods of Detection
- ▪ Overview of Stack-Based Buffer Overflows
- ▪ Overview of Buffer Overflow Mutation Techniques

 SQL injection and buffer overflows are similar exploits in that they're both usually delivered via a user-input field. The input field is where a user may enter a username and password on a website, add data to a URL, or perform a search for a keyword in another application.

Both SQL server injection and buffer overflow vulnerabilities are caused by the same issue: invalid parameters. If programmers don't take the time to validate the variables a user can enter into a variable field, the results can be serious and unpredictable. Sophisticated hackers can exploit this vulnerability, causing an execution fault and shutdown of the system or application, or a command shell to be executed for the hacker.

SQL Injection

As a CEH, it's important for you to be able to define SQL injection and understand the steps a hacker takes to conduct a SQL injection attack. In addition, you should know SQL server vulnerabilities, as well as countermeasures to SQL injection attacks.

We'll discuss these in the following sections.

What Is SQL Injection?

During a *SQL injection* attack, malicious code is inserted into a web form field or the website's code to make a system execute a command shell or other arbitrary commands. Just as a legitimate user enters queries and additions to the SQL database via a web form, the hacker can insert commands to the SQL server through the same web form field. For example, an arbitrary command from a hacker might open a command prompt or display a table from the database. A database table may contain personal information such as credit card numbers, social security numbers, or passwords. SQL servers are very common database servers and used by many organizations to store confidential data. This makes a SQL server a high value target and therefore a system that is very attractive to hackers.

Understand the Steps to Conduct SQL Injection

Before launching a SQL injection attack, the hacker determines whether the configuration of the database and related tables and variables is vulnerable. The steps to determine the SQL server's vulnerability are as follows:

1. Using your web browser, search for a website that uses a login page or other database input or query fields (such as an "I forgot my password" form). Look for web pages that display the POST or GET HTML commands by checking the site's source code.

2. Test the SQL server using single quotes (' '). Doing so indicates whether the user-input variable is sanitized or interpreted literally by the server. If the server responds with an error message that says *use 'a'='a'* (or something similar), then it's most likely susceptible to a SQL injection attack.

3. Use the SELECT command to retrieve data from the database or the INSERT command to add information to the database.

Understand SQL Server Vulnerabilities

Here are some examples of variable field text you can use on a web form to test for SQL vulnerabilities:

- `Blah' or 1=1--`
- `Login:blah' or 1=1--`
- `Password::blah' or 1=1--`
- `http://search/index.asp?id=blah' or 1=1--`

These commands and similar variations may allow the bypassing of a login depending on the structure of the database. When entered in a form field the commands may return many rows in a table or even an entire database table because the SQL server is interpreting the terms literally. The double dashes near the end of the command tell SQL to ignore the rest of the command as a comment.

Here are some examples of how to use SQL commands to take control.

To get a directory listing, type the following in a form field:

```
Blah';exec master..xp_cmdshell "dir c:\*.* /s >c:\directory.txt"--
```

To create a file, type the following in a form field:

```
Blah';exec master..xp_cmdshell "echo hacker-was-here > c:\hacker.txt"--
```

To ping an IP address, type the following in a form field:

```
Blah';exec master..xp_cmdshell "ping 192.168.1.1"--
```

Describe SQL Injection Countermeasures

The first countermeasures to prevent a SQL injection attack are to minimize the privileges of a user's connection to the database and to enforce strong passwords for SA and Administrator accounts. You should also disable verbose or explanatory error messages so no more information than necessary is sent to the hacker (such information can help them determine whether the SQL server is vulnerable).

It's critical to review source code for the following programming weaknesses:

- Single quotes
- Lack of input validation

Some countermeasures to SQL injection are:

- Rejecting known bad input
- Checking input bounds

Buffer Overflows

As a CEH, you must be able to identify different types of buffer overflows. You should also know how to detect a buffer overflow vulnerability and understand the steps a hacker may use to perform a stack-based overflow attack. We'll look at these topics, as well as an overview of buffer-overflow mutation techniques, in the following sections.

Identify the Different Types of Buffer Overflows and Methods of Detection

Buffer overflows are exploits that hackers use against an operating system or application; like SQL injection attacks, they're usually targeted at user input fields. A buffer overflow exploit causes a system to fail by overloading memory or executing a command shell or arbitrary code on the target system. A buffer-overflow vulnerability is caused by a lack of bounds checking or a lack of input-validation sanitization in a variable field (such as on a web form). If the application doesn't check or validate the size or format of a variable before sending it to be stored in memory, an overflow vulnerability exits.

The two types of buffer overflows are stack-based and heap-based. The *stack* and the *heap* are storage locations for user-supplied variables within a running program. Variables are stored in the stack or heap until the program needs them. Stacks are static locations of memory address space, whereas heaps are dynamic memory address spaces that occur while a program is running. A heap-based buffer overflow occurs in the lower part of the memory and over-writes other dynamic variables. As a consequence, a program can open a shell or command prompt or stop the execution of a program. The next section describes stack-based buffer overflow attacks.

To detect program buffer overflow vulnerabilities that result from poorly written source code, a hacker sends large amounts of data to the application via a form field and sees what the program does as a result.

Overview of Stack-Based Buffer Overflows

The following are the steps a hacker uses to execute a stack-based buffer overflow:

1. Enter a variable into the buffer to exhaust the amount of memory in the stack.
2. Enter more data than the buffer has allocated in memory for that variable, which causes the memory to overflow or run into the memory space for the next process. Then, add

another variable, and overwrite the return pointer that tells the program where to return to after executing the variable.

3. A program executes this malicious code variable and then uses the return pointer to get back to the next line of executable code. If the hacker successfully overwrites the pointer, then the program executes the hacker's code instead of the program code.

Most hackers don't need to be this familiar with the details of buffer overflows. Prewritten exploits can be found on the Internet and are exchanged between hacker groups.

 The memory register that gets overwritten with the return address of the exploit code is known as the EIP

Overview of Buffer Overflow Mutation Techniques

As you see, hackers can graduate from standard buffer overflows to redirecting the return pointer to the code of their choosing. A hacker must know the exact memory address and the size of the stack in order to make the return pointer execute their code. A hacker can use a No Operation (NOP) instruction, which is just padding to move the instruction pointer and does not execute any code. The NOP is added to a string before the malicious code to be executed.

If an intrusion detection system (IDS) is present on the network, it can thwart a hacker who sends a series of NOPs to forward the instruction pointer. To bypass the IDS, the hacker can randomly replace some of the NOPs with equivalent pieces of code, such as x++,x-;?NOPNOP. This example of a mutated buffer overflow attack can bypass detection by an IDS.

Programmers should not use the built-in strcpy(), strcat(), and streadd() C/C++ Functions as these are susceptible to buffer overflows. Alternately Java can be used as the programming language as Java is not susceptible to buffer overflows.

Exam Essentials

Understand how SQL injection and buffer overflow attacks are similar.   SQL injection and buffer overflows are similar in that both attacks are delivered via a web form field.

Understand SQL injection countermeasures.   Utilizing correct programming code without single quotes and performing bounds-checking and input validation are SQL injection countermeasures.

Know the difference between a stack-based and a heap-based buffer overflow.   Stacks are static locations of memory address space, whereas heaps are dynamic memory address spaces.

Understand how to bypass an IDS using a buffer overflow attack.   An IDS looks for a series of NOPs. By replacing the NOP with other code segments, a hacker can effectively bypass an IDS.

Understand buffer overflow and SQL injection countermeasures.   Bounds-checking and sanitizing the input from a web form can prevent a buffer overflow and SQL injection vulnerability.

Review Questions

1. Entering **Password::blah** ' or **1=1-** into a web form in order to get a password is an example of what type of attack?

   A. Buffer overflow

   B. Heap-based overflow

   C. Stack-based overflow

   D. SQL injection

2. Replacing NOPs with other code in a buffer-overflow mutation serves what purpose?

   A. Bypassing an IDS

   B. Overwriting the return pointer

   C. Advancing the return pointer

   D. Bypassing a firewall

3. Which of the following is used to store dynamically allocated variables?

   A. Heap overflow

   B. Stack overflow

   C. Heap

   D. Stack

4. What is the first step in a SQL injection attack?

   A. Enter arbitrary commands at a user prompt.

   B. Locate a user input field on a web page.

   C. Locate the return pointer.

   D. Enter a series of NOPs.

5. What command is used to retrieve information from a SQL database?

   A. INSERT

   B. GET

   C. SET

   D. SELECT

6. Which of the following is a countermeasure for buffer overflows?

   A. Not using single quotes

   B. Securing all login pages with SSL

   C. Bounds checking

   D. User validation

7. What does NOP stand for?

   A. No Operation

   B. Network Operation Protocol

   C. No Once Prompt

   D. Network Operation

8. A hacker needs to be familiar with the memory address space and techniques of buffer overflows in order to launch a buffer overflow attack.

   A. True

   B. False

9. Why are many programs vulnerable to SQL injection and buffer overflow attacks?

   A. The programs are written quickly and use poor programming techniques.

   B. These are inherent flaws in any program.

   C. The users have not applied the correct service packs.

   D. The programmers are using the wrong programming language.

10. Which command would a hacker enter in a web form field to obtain a directory listing?

   A. `Blah';exec master..xp_cmdshell "dir *.*"--`

   B. `Blah';exec_cmdshell "dir c:\*.* /s >c:\directory.txt"--`

   C. `Blah';exec master..xp_cmdshell "dir c:\*.* /s >c:\directory.txt"--`

   D. `Blah';exec cmdshell "dir c:\*.* "--`

11. What are two types of buffer overflow attacks?

   A. Heap and stack

   B. Heap and overflow

   C. Stack and memory allocation

   D. Injection and heap

Answers to Review Questions

1. D. Use of a single quote indicates a SQL injection attack.

2. A. The purpose of mutating a buffer overflow by replacing NOPs is to bypass an IDS.

3. C. A heap is using to store dynamic variables.

4. B. The first step in a SQL injection attack is to locate a user input field on a web page using a web browser.

5. D. The command to retrieve information from a SQL database is SELECT.

6. C. Performing bounds checking is a countermeasure for buffer overflow attacks.

7. A. NOP is an acronym for No Operation.

8. B, False. A hacker can run a prewritten exploit to launch a buffer overflow.

9. A. Programs can be exploited because they're written quickly and poorly.

10. C. `Blah';exec master..xp_cmdshell "dir c:\*.* /s >c:\directory.txt"--` is the command to obtain a directory listing utilizing SQL injection.

11. A. Heap and stack are the two types of buffer overflows.

Chapter

10

Wireless Hacking

CEH EXAM OBJECTIVES COVERED IN THIS CHAPTER:

- ✓ Overview of WEP, WPA Authentication Mechanisms, and Cracking Techniques
- ✓ Overview of Wireless Sniffers and Locating SSIDs, MAC Spoofing
- ✓ Understand Rogue Access Points
- ✓ Understand Wireless Hacking Techniques
- ✓ Describe the Methods Used to Secure Wireless Networks

Wireless networks add another entry point into a network for hackers. Much has been written about wireless security and hacking because wireless is a relatively new technology and ripe with security holes. Because of the broadcast nature of Radio Frequency (RF) wireless networks and the rapid adoption of wireless technologies for home and business networks, many vulnerabilities and exploits exist.

Most wireless LANs (WLANs) are based on the IEEE 802.11 standards and amendments, such as 802.11a, 802.11b, 802.11g, and 802.11n. The 802.11 standard included only rudimentary security features and was fraught with vulnerabilities. The 802.11i amendment is the latest security solution that addresses the 802.11 weaknesses. The Wi-Fi Alliance created additional security certifications known as *Wi-Fi Protected Access* (WPA) and WPA2 to fill the gap between the original 802.11 standard and the latest 802.11i amendment. The security vulnerabilities and security solutions discussed in this chapter are all based on these IEEE and Wi-Fi Alliance standards.

Overview of WEP, WPA Authentication Mechanisms, and Cracking Techniques

Two methods exist for authenticating wireless LAN clients to an access point: open system or shared key authentication. Open system does not provide any security mechanisms but is simply a request to make a connection to the network. Shared key authentication has the wireless client hash a string of challenge text with the WEP key to authenticate to the network. The details of WEP will be discussed further in the following section.

Wired Equivalent Privacy (WEP) was the first security option for 802.11 WLANs. WEP is used to encrypt data on the WLAN and can optionally be paired with shared key authentication to authenticate WLAN clients. WEP uses an RC4 64-bit or 128-bit encryption key to encrypt the layer 2 data payload. This WEP key comprises a 40-bit or 104-bit user-defined key combined with a 24-bit Initialization Vector (IV), making the WEP key either 64- or 128-bit.

The process by which RC4 uses IVs is the real weakness of WEP: It allows a hacker to crack the WEP key. The method, knows as the *FMS attack*, uses encrypted output bytes to determine the most probable key bytes. It was incorporated into products like AirSnort, WEPCrack, and aircrack to exploit the WEP vulnerability. Although a hacker can attempt to crack WEP by brute force, the most common technique is the FMS attack.

WPA employs the Temporal Key Integrity Protocol (TKIP)—which is a safer RC4 implementation—for data encryption and either WPA Personal or WPA Enterprise for authentication. WPA Personal uses an ASCII passphrase for authentication while WPA Enterprise uses a RADIUS server to authenticate users. WPA Enterprise is a more secure robust security option but relies on the creation and more complex setup of a RADIUS server. TKIP rotates the data encryption key to prevent the vulnerabilities of WEP and, consequently, cracking attacks. WPA2 is similar to 802.11i and uses the Advanced Encryption Standard (AES) to encrypt the data payload. AES is considered an uncrackable encryption algorithm. WPA2 also allows for the use of TKIP during a transitional period called *mixed mode security*. This transitional mode means both TKIP and AES can be used to encrypt data. AES requires a faster processor, which means low-end devices like PDAs may only support TKIP. WPA Personal and WPA2 Personal use a passphrase to authentication WLAN clients. WPA Enterprise and WPA2 Enterprise authenticate WLAN users via a RADIUS server using the 802.1X/Extensible Authentication Protocol (EAP) standards.

802.11i and WPA2 use the same encryption and authentication mechanisms as WPA2. However, WPA2 doesn't require vendors to implement preauthorization. Preauthorization enables fast, secure roaming, which is necessary in very mobile environments with time-sensitive applications such as wireless voice over IP.

Table 10.1 summarizes the authentication and encryption options for WLANs.

TABLE 10.1   802.11 and WPA Security Solutions and Weaknesses

	Encryption	Authentication	Weakness
Original IEEE 802.11 standard	WEP	WEP	IV weakness allows the WEP key to be cracked. The same key is used for encryption and authentication of all clients to the WLAN.
WPA	TKIP	Passphrase or RADIUS (802.1x/EAP)	Passphrase is susceptible to a dictionary attack.
WPA2	AES (can use TKIP while in mixed mode)	Passphrase or RADIUS (802.1x/EAP)	Passphrase is susceptible to a dictionary attack.
IEEE 802.11i	AES (can use TKIP while in mixed mode)	Passphrase or RADIUS (802.1x/EAP)	Passphrase is susceptible to a dictionary attack.

Hacking Tools

Aircrack is a WEP-cracking software tool. It doesn't capture packets; it's used to perform the cracking after another tool has captured the encrypted packets. Aircrack runs on Windows or Linux.

WEPCrack and AirSnort are Linux-based WEP-cracking tools.

NetStumbler and Kismet are WLAN discovery tools. They both discover the Media Access Control (MAC) address, Service Set Identifier (SSID), security mode, and channel of the WLAN. Additionally, Kismet can discover WLANs whose SSIDs are hidden, collect packets, and provide IDS functionality.

Overview of Wireless Sniffers and Locating SSIDs, MAC Spoofing

A common attack on a WLAN involves eavesdropping or sniffing. This is an easy attack to perform and usually occurs at hotspots or with any default installation access point (AP), because packets are generally sent unencrypted across the WLAN. Passwords for network access protocols such as FTP, POP3, and SMTP can be captured in clear text, meaning unencrypted, by a hacker on an unencrypted WLAN.

The SSID is the name of the WLAN and can be located in a beacon. If two wireless networks are physically close, the SSIDs are used to identify and differentiate the respective networks. The SSID is usually sent in the clear in a beacon packet. Most APs allow the WLAN administrator to hide the SSID. However, this isn't a robust security mechanism because some tools can read the SSID from other packets such as probe and data packets.

An early security solution in WLAN technology used MAC address filters: A network administrator entered a list of valid MAC addresses for the systems allowed to associate with the AP. MAC filters are cumbersome to configure and aren't scaleable for an enterprise network because they must be configured on each AP. MAC spoofing is easy to perform and negates the effort required to implement MAC filters. A hacker can identify a valid MAC address because the MAC headers are never encrypted.

Hacking Tool

SMAC is a MAC spoofing tool that a hacker can use to spoof a valid user's address and gain access to the network.

Understand Rogue Access Points

Rogue access points are WLAN access points that aren't authorized to connect to a target network. Rogue APs open a wireless hole into the network. A hacker can plant a rogue AP, or an employee may unknowingly create a security hole by plugging an access point into the network so the user can be mobile. Any rogue AP can be used by anyone who can connect to the AP, including a hacker, giving them access to the wired LAN. This is why it's critical for organizations that have a no wireless policy to perform wireless scanning to ensure no rogue APs are connected to the network.

Understand Wireless Hacking Techniques

Most wireless hacking attacks can be categorized as follows:

Cracking encryption and authentication mechanisms   These mechanisms include cracking WEP, WPA preshared key authentication passphrase, and Cisco's Lightweight EAP authentication (LEAP). Hackers can use them to connect to the WLAN using stolen credentials or can capture other users' data and decrypt/encrypt it.

Eavesdropping or sniffing   This involves capturing passwords or other confidential information from an unencrypted WLAN or hotspot.

Denial of Service   DoS can be performed at the physical layer by creating a louder RF signature than the AP with an RF transmitter, causing an approved AP to fail so users connect to a rogue AP. DoS can be performed at the Logical Link Control (LLC) layer by generating deauthentication frames (deauth attacks) or by continuously generating bogus frames (Queensland attack).

AP masquerading or spoofing   Rogue APs pretend to be legitimate APs by using the same configuration SSID settings or network name.

MAC spoofing   The hacker pretends to be a legitimate WLAN client and bypasses MAC filters by spoofing another user's MAC address.

Wireless networks give a hacker an easy way into the network if the AP isn't secured properly. There are many ways to hack or exploit the vulnerabilities of a WLAN.

Describe the Methods Used to Secure Wireless Networks

Because wireless networking is a relatively new technology compared to wired networking technologies, fewer security options are available. Security methods can be categorized by the applicable layer of the OSI model.

Layer 2 or MAC layer security options are as follows:

- WPA
- WPA2
- 802.11i

Layer 3 or Network layer security options are as follows:

- IPSec or SSL VPN

Layer 7 or Application layer security options are as follows:

- Secure applications such as Secure Shell (SSH), HTTP Over SSL (HTTPS), and FTP/SSL (FTPS)

 Because of its numerous weaknesses, WEP shouldn't be used as the sole security mechanism for a WLAN.

Exam Essentials

Understand the inherent security vulnerabilities of using a WLAN.   RF is a broadcast medium, and therefore all traffic is able to be captured by a hacker.

Understand the security solutions implemented in the IEEE 802.11 standard.   WEP, shared key, and MAC filters are security solutions offered in the original IEEE 802.11 standard.

Understand the security solutions offered by the Wi-Fi Alliance.   WPA and WPA2 are Wi-Fi Alliance equipment security certifications.

Know what an SSID is used for on a WLAN.   The SSID identifies the network name and shouldn't be used as a security mechanism.

Know what security mechanisms should not be used for WLAN security.   WEP and MAC filters shouldn't be used as the sole means to secure the WLAN.

Review Questions

1. Which of the following security solutions uses the same key for both encryption and authentication?

   A. WPA

   B. WPA2

   C. WEP

   D. 802.11i

2. WEP stands for what?

   A. Wireless Encryption Protocol

   B. Wired Equivalent Privacy

   C. Wireless Encryption Privacy

   D. Wired Encryption Protocol

3. What makes WEP crackable?

   A. Same key used for encryption and authentication

   B. Length of the key

   C. Weakness of IV

   D. RC4

4. Which form of encryption does WPA use?

   A. AES

   B. TKIP

   C. LEAP

   D. Shared key

5. Which form of authentication does WPA2 use?

   A. Passphrase only

   B. 802.1x/EAP/RADIUS

   C. Passphrase or 802.1x/EAP/RADIUS

   D. AES

6. 802.11i is most similar to which wireless security standard?

   A. WPA2

   B. WPA

   C. TKIP

   D. AES

7. Which of the following is a layer 3 security solution for WLANs?

A. MAC filter

B. WEP

C. WPA

D. VPN

8. A device that sends deauth frames is performing which type of attack against the WLAN?

A. Denial of Service

B. Cracking

C. Sniffing

D. MAC spoofing

9. The most dangerous type of attack against a WLAN is _____.

A. WEP cracking

B. Rogue access point

C. Eavesdropping

D. MAC spoofing

10. 802.11i is implemented at which layer of the OSI model?

A. Layer 1

B. Layer 2

C. Layer 3

D. Layer 7

- Opportunity to plant rogue access points to create an open wireless network with access to the wired network
- Theft of paper or electronic documents
- Theft of sensitive fax information
- Dumpster diving attack (emphasizing the need to shred important documents)

Understanding Physical Security

Generally security measures can be categorized in the following three ways:

Physical   Physical measures to prevent access to systems include security guards, lighting, fences, locks, and alarms. Facility access points should be limited, and they should be monitored/protected by closed-circuit television (CCTV) cameras and alarms. The entrance to the facility should be restricted to authorized people. Access to laptop systems and removable media such as removable drives, backup tapes, and disks should be restricted and protected. Computer screens should be positioned such that they can't be seen by passers-by, and a policy should be implemented and enforced that requires users to lock their systems when they leave the computer for any reason. Computer systems with highly sensitive data should be protected in an enclosed and locked area such as a credential-access room with a rack-mount case and lock.

Technical   Technical security measures such as firewalls, IDS, spyware content filtering, and virus and Trojan scanning should be implemented on all remote client systems, networks, and servers.

Operational   Operational security measures to analyze threats and perform risk assessments should be a documented process in the organization's security policy.

Technical and Operational security measures are dealt with in other chapters of this book.

What Is the Need for Physical Security?

You need physical security measures for the same reason you need other types of security (such as technical or operational) to prevent hackers from gaining access to your network and your information. A hacker can easily get such access through weaknesses in physical security measures. In addition, data can be lost or damaged by natural causes; so, risk managers must add natural disasters to the equation when planning appropriate security. Physical security measures are designed to prevent the following:

- Unauthorized access to a computer system
- Stealing of data from systems
- Corruption of data stored on a system
- Loss of data or damage to systems caused by natural causes

Who Is Accountable for Physical Security?

The following people in an organization should be accountable for physical security:

- The organization's physical security officer
- Information system professionals
- Chief information officer
- Employees

   Everyone in an organization is responsible for enforcing physical security policies. It's the physical security officer's responsibility to set the physical security standard and implement physical security measures.

Factors Affecting Physical Security

Physical security is affected by factors outside the physical security controls. Factors that can affect an organization's physical security include the following:

- Vandalism
- Theft
- Natural causes, such as
  - Earthquake
  - Fire
  - Flood

   Security professionals need to be aware of these risk factors and plan accordingly. Many organizations create a business continuity plan (BCP) or disaster recovery plan (DRP) to prepare for these possibilities.

Exam Essentials

Understand the attacks that can be performed via physical access.   Physical access gives a hacker the ability to perform password cracking, rogue wireless access points and theft of equipment attacks.

Understand the important role physical security plays in an organization's security plan. Physical security is critical to an organization's security plan.

Know some factors that affect the enforcement of physical security.   Vandalism, theft, and natural causes affect the enforcement of physical security.

Know who is accountable for physical security.   The organization's security officer, information system professionals, chief information officer, and employees are responsible for physical security.

Understand the need for physical security.   Physical security is necessary to prevent unauthorized access to a building or computer system, theft of data, corruption of data stored on a system, and loss of data or damage to systems caused by natural causes.

Review Questions

1. Who is responsible for implementing physical security? (Choose all that apply.)

    A. The owner of the company

    B. Chief information officer

    C. IT managers

    D. Employees

2. What factor does impact physical security?

    A. Encryption in use on the network

    B. Flood or fire

    C. IDS implementation

    D. Configuration of firewall

3. Physical security is designed to prevent what?

    A. Stealing confidential data

    B. Hacking systems from the inside

    C. Hacking systems from the Internet

    D. Physical access

4. Which of the following is often one of the most overlooked areas of security?

    A. Operational

    B. Technical

    C. Internet

    D. Physical

5. A hacker who plants a rogue wireless access point on a network in order to sniff the traffic on the wired network from outside the building is causing what type of security breach?

    A. Physical

    B. Technical

    C. Operational

    D. Remote access

6. Which area of security usually receives the least amount of attention during a penetration test?

    A. Technical

    B. Physical

    C. Operational

    D. Wireless

7. Which of the following attacks can be perpetrated by a hacker against an organization with weak physical security controls?

   A. Denial of service

   B. Radio frequency jamming

   C. Hardware keylogger

   D. Banner grabbing

8. Which type of access allows passwords stored on a local system to be cracked?

   A. Physical

   B. Technical

   C. Remote

   D. Dial-in

9. Which of the following is an example of a physical security breach?

   A. Capturing a credit card number from a web server application

   B. Hacking a SQL server in order to locate a credit card number

   C. Stealing a laptop to acquire credit card numbers

   D. Sniffing a credit card number from packets sent on a wireless hotspot

10. What type of attack can be performed once a hacker has physical access?

   A. Finding passwords by dumpster diving

   B. Stealing equipment

   C. Performing a DoS attack

   D. Session hijacking

Answers to Review Questions

1.   A, B, C, D. The chief information officer, along with all the employees, is responsible for implementing physical security.

2.   B. A fire or flood are factors that can affect physical security while all the others are technical security issues.

3.   A, B, D. Physical security is designed to prevent stealing of confidential data, hacking systems from the inside, and physical access restricted to authorized personnel. Technical security defends against hacking systems from the Internet.

4.   D. Physical security is one of the most overlooked areas of security.

5.   A. In order to place a wireless access point, a hacker needs to have physical access.

6.   B. Physical security usually receives the least amount of testing during a penetration test.

7.   C. A hardware keylogger can be installed to capture passwords or other confidential data once a hacker gains physical access to a client system.

8.   A. Physical access allows a hacker to crack passwords on a local system.

9.   C. Theft of equipment is an example of a physical security breach.

10. B. Stealing equipment requires physical access.

Chapter

12

Linux Hacking

CEH EXAM OBJECTIVES COVERED IN THIS CHAPTER:

- ✓ Linux Basics
- ✓ Understand How to Compile a Linux Kernel
- ✓ Understand GCC Compilation Commands
- ✓ Understand How to Install Linux Kernel Modules
- ✓ Understand Linux Hardening Methods

Linux is a popular operating system with systems administrators because of its open source code and its flexibility, which allows anyone to modify it. Because of the open source nature of Linux, there are many different versions, known as *distributions* (or *distros*). Several of the Linux distributions have become robust commercial operating systems for use on workstations as well as servers. Popular commercial distributions include Red Hat, Debian, Mandrake, and SUSE; some of the most common free versions are Gentoo and Knoppix.

Linux's flexibility and cost, together with the increase in Linux applications, have made it the operating system of choice for many systems. Although Linux has inherently tighter security than Windows operating systems, it also has vulnerabilities that can be exploited. This chapter covers the basics of getting started using Linux as an operating system and knowing how to harden the system to attacks.

Linux Basics

Linux is loosely based on UNIX and anyone familiar working in a UNIX environment should be able to use a Linux system. All standard commands and utilities are included on most distros.

Many text editors are available inside a Linux system, including vi, ex, pico, jove, and GNU emacs. Many UNIX users prefer "simple" editors like vi. But vi has many limitations due to its age, and most modern editors like emacs have gained popularity in recent years.

Most of the basic Linux utilities are GNU software, meaning they are freely distributed to the community. GNU utilities also support advanced features that are not found in the standard versions of BSD and UNIX System. However, GNU utilities are intended to remain compatible with BSD.

A shell is a command-line program interface that allows a user to enter commands and the system executes commands from the user. In addition, many shells provide features like job control, managing several processes at once, input and output redirection, and a command language for writing shell scripts. A shell script is a program written in the shell's command language and is similar to a MS-DOS batch file.

Many types of shells are available for Linux. The most important difference between shells is the command language. For example, the C SHell (csh) uses a command language similar to the C programming language. The classic Bourne SHell (sh) uses another command language. The choice of a shell is often based on the command language it provides, and determines which features will be available to the user.

The GNU Bourne Again Shell (bash) is a variation of the Bourne Shell which includes many advanced features like job control, command history, command and filename completion, and an interface for editing files. Another popular shell is tcsh, a version of the C Shell with advanced functionality similar to that found in bash. Other shells include zsh, a small Bourne-like shell; the Korn Shell (ksh); BSD's ash; and rc, the Plan 9 shell.

Understand How to Compile a Linux Kernel

Because of the open source nature of Linux, the source code is freely distributed. The source code is available as binary files, which must be compiled in order to properly operate as an operating system. The binary files are available to anyone and may be downloaded and modified to add or change functionality. There are three reasons a user might want to recompile the Linux kernel. Firstly, you may have some hardware that is so new that there's no kernel module for it in on your distribution CD. Secondly, you may have come across some kind of bug which is fixed in a revision of the operating system. Lastly, you may have some new software application which requires a newer version of the operating system

This is great for flexibility, but users should beware of sites from which the source code is downloaded because that may have bad or infected code, Trojans, or other backdoors added to the source code. For security reasons, only download Linux from known and trusted Internet websites or purchase a commercial distro.

 The recommended site to download the Linux kernel from is `ftp.kernel.org`.

To download, configure, and compile the Linux kernel, follow these steps:

1. Locate the file for the latest version of the operating system and download it to the /usr/src directory on the Linux system. Then use the `tar zxf` command to unpack it.

2. The next step is to configure the Linux kernel. Change directory to /usr/src/Linux and type make `menuconfig`. This will build a few programs and then quickly pop up a window. The window menu lets you alter many aspects of kernel configuration. After you have made any necessary changes, save the configuration and type `make dep; make clean`. The first of these commands builds the tree of interdependencies in the kernel sources. These dependencies may have been affected by the options you have chosen in the configure step. The `make clean` purges any unwanted files left from previous builds of the kernel.

3. The next commands, `make zImage` and `make modules`, may take a long time because they are compiling the kernel.

4. The last step is installing the new kernel. On an Intel-based system the kernel is installed in /boot with the command:

```
cp /usr/Linux/src/arch/i386/boot/zImage /boot/newkernel
```

5. Then use the command `make modules_install`. This will install the modules in /lib/ modules.

6. Next, edit /etc/lilo.conf to add a section like this:

```
image = /boot/newkernel
label = new
read-only
```

7. At the next reboot, select the new kernel in lilo and it will load the new kernel. If it works, move it to the first position in the lilo.conf so it will boot every time by default.

> Linux live CDs are a good choice if you're new to Linux. Using the live CD, you can test and use the operating system without installing Linux on the system. To use a live CD, visit www.distrowatch.com to choose a distribution. Then, download the ISO file, and write it to a CD. That CD can be put in any system and booted to a fully functioning version of Linux.

Understand GCC Compilation Commands

GNU Compiler Collection (GCC) is a command-line compiler that takes source code and makes it an executable. You can download it from http://gcc.gnu.org (many Linux distributions also include a version of GCC). GCC can be used to compile and execute C, C++, and Fortran applications so they are able to run on a Linux system.

The following command compiles C++ code with the GCC for use as an application:

```
g++ filename.cpp -o outputfilename.out
```

The command to compile C code with the GCC for use as an application is as follows:

```
gcc filename.c -o outputfilename.out
```

Understand How to Install Linux Kernel Modules

Linux Kernel Modules (LKMs) let you add functionality to the operating system without having to recompile the OS.

A danger of using LKMs is that a rootkit can easily be created as an LKM and, if loaded, it infects the kernel. For this reason, you should download LKMs only from a verified good source.

Examples of LKM rootkits are Knark, Adore, and Rtkit. Because they infect the kernel, these rootkits are more difficult to detect than those that do not manifest themselves as LKMs. Once a system has been compromised, the hacker can put the LKM in the `/tmp` or the `/var/tmp` directory, which can't be monitored by the system administrator, thereby hiding processes, files, and network connections. System calls can also be replaced with those of the hacker's choosing on a system infected by an LKM rootkit.

The command to load a LKM is `modprobe LKM`.

Understand Linux Hardening Methods

Hardening is the process of improving security on a system by making modifications to the system. Linux can be made more secure by employing some of these hardening methods.

The first step in securing any server, Linux or Windows, is to ensure that it's in a secure location such as a network operations center, which prevents a hacker from gaining physical access to the system.

The next and most obvious security measure is to use strong passwords and not give out usernames or passwords. Administrators should make sure the system doesn't have null passwords by verifying that all user accounts have passwords in the `/etc/shadow` file.

The default security stance of `deny all` is a good one for hardening a system from a network attack. After applying `deny all`, the administrator can open certain access for specific users. By using the `deny all` command first, the administrator ensures that users aren't being given access to files that they shouldn't have access to. The command to deny all users access from the network is

```
Cat "All:All">> /etc/hosts.deny
```

Another good way to harden a Linux server is to remove unused services and ensure that the system is patched with the latest bug fixes. Administrators should also check system logs frequently for anything unusual that could indicate an attack.

The following are other recommended steps to improve the security of a Linux server:

- Use a widely recognized and known good Linux distribution.
- Don't install unnecessary applications or services.
- Change the default passwords.
- Disable remote root login.
- Set up and enable IP tables.
- Install a host-based intrusion detection system (HIDS).
- Utilize log files.

Exam Essentials

Understand the use of Linux in the marketplace. Linux has become more popular with the introduction of commercial versions and more available applications. Linux can be used as a hacking platform, as a server, or as a workstation.

Know how to use a Linux live CD. Locate and download an ISO file. Write it to a CD, and boot a system from the CD to use the Linux operating system.

Know the steps to create a Linux operating system. Locate and download the binary files, and compile the Linux source files; then, install the compiled OS.

Know how to harden a Linux system. Use a known good distribution, change the default passwords, disable the root login, use IP tables, use an HIDS, apply the latest fixes, and monitor log files to harden a Linux system.

Understand how LKMs are used. LKMs add functionality to a Linux system, but they should be used only from a known good source.

Know about GCC compilation. GCC compilers are used to create executable applications from C or C++ source code.

Review Questions

1. What does LKM stand for?

   A. Linux Kernel Module

   B. Linux Kernel Mode

   C. Linked Kernel Module

   D. Last Kernel Mode

2. What GCC command is used to compile a C++ file called `source` into an executable file called `game`?

   A. `g++ source.c -o game`

   B. `gcc source.c -o game`

   C. `gcc make source.cpp -o game`

   D. `g++ source.cpp -o game`

3. What is the command to deny all users access from the network?

   A. `Cat "All:All">> /etc/hosts.deny`

   B. `Set "All:All">> /etc/hosts.deny`

   C. `IP deny "All:All"`

   D. `Cat All:All deny`

4. Of the following, which are common commercial Linux distributions?

   A. SUSE, Knark, and Red Hat

   B. SUSE, Adore, Debian, and Mandrake

   C. SUSE, Debian, and Red Hat

   D. SUSE, Adore, and Red Hat

5. What is a Linux live CD?

   A. A Linux operating system that runs from CD

   B. A Linux operating system installed from a CD onto a hard drive

   C. A Linux tool that runs applications from a CD

   D. A Linux application that makes CDs

6. What type of attack can be disguised as an LKM?

   A. DoS

   B. Trojan

   C. Spam virus

   D. Rootkit

7. Which of the following is a reason to use Linux?

A. Linux has no security holes.

B. Linux is always up to date on security patches.

C. No rootkits can infect a Linux system.

D. Linux is flexible and can be modified.

8. Which of the following is not a way to harden Linux?

A. Physically secure the system.

B. Maintain a current patch level.

C. Change the default passwords.

D. Install all available services.

9. What type of file is used to create a Linux live CD?

A. ISO

B. CD

C. LIN

D. CDFS

10. Why is it important to use a known good distribution of Linux?

A. Source files can become corrupt if not downloaded properly.

B. Only certain distributions can be patched.

C. Source files can be modified, and a Trojan or backdoor may be included in the source binaries of some less-known or free distributions of Linux.

D. Only some versions of Linux are available to the public.

Answers to Review Questions

1. A. LKM stands for Linux Kernel Module.

2. D. `g++ source.cpp -o game` is the GCC command to create an executable called game from the source file `source`.

3. A. `Cat "All:All" /etc/hosts.deny` is the command to deny all users access from the network on a Linux system.

4. C. SUSE, Debian, and Red Hat are all commercial versions of Linux.

5. A. A Linux live CD is a fully functioning operating system that runs from a CD.

6. D. A rootkit can be disguised as an LKM.

7. D. Linux is flexible and can be modified because the source code is openly available.

8. D. Linux should not have unused services running, because each additional service may have potential vulnerabilities.

9. A. An ISO file is used to create a Linux live CD.

10. C. Known good distributions have been reviewed by the Linux community to verify that a Trojan or backdoor does not exist in the source code.

Evading IDSs, Honeypots, and Firewalls

CEH EXAM OBJECTIVES COVERED IN THIS CHAPTER:

✓ List the Types of Intrusion Detection Systems and Evasion Techniques

✓ List the Firewall Types and Honeypot Evasion Techniques

Intrusion Detection Systems (IDS), firewalls, and honeypots are all security measures used to ensure a hacker is not able to gain access to a network or target system. An IDS and a firewall are both essentially packet filtering devices and are used to monitor traffic based upon a predefined set of rules. A honeypot is a fake target system used to lure hackers away from the more valuable targets. As with other security mechanisms, IDSs, firewalls and honeypots are only as good as their design and implementation. It is important to be familiar with how these devices operate and provide security as they are commonly subjects of attack.

List the Types of Intrusion Detection Systems and Evasion Techniques

Intrusion detection systems (IDSs) are systems that inspect traffic and look for known signatures of attacks or unusual behavior patterns. A *packet-sniffer* views and monitors traffic and is a built-in component of an IDS. An IDS alerts a command center or system administrator by pager, e-mail or cell phone when an event listed on the company's security event list is triggered. *Intrusion prevention systems* (IPSs) initiate countermeasures such as blocking traffic when suspected traffic flow is detected. IPS systems automate the response to an intrusion attempt and allow you to automate the deny-access capability.

There are two main types of IDS:

Host-based   Host-based IDSs (HIDSs) are applications that reside on a single system or host and filter traffic or events based on a known signature list for that specific operating system. HIDSs include Norton Internet Security and Cisco Security Agent (CSA). Warning: Many worms and Trojans can turn off an HIDS.

Network-based   Network-based IDSs (NIDSs) are software-based appliances that reside on the network. They're used solely for intrusion detection purposes to detect all types of malicious network traffic and computer usage that can't be detected by a conventional firewall. This includes network attacks against vulnerable services, data attacks on applications, host-based attacks such as privilege escalation, unauthorized logins and access to sensitive files, and malware. NIDSs are *passive* systems; the IDS sensor detects a potential security breach, logs the information, and signals an alert on the console.

Hacking Tool

Snort is a real-time packet sniffer, HIDS, and traffic-logging tool deployed on Linux and Windows systems. You can configure Snort and the IDS rules in the `snort.conf` file. The command to install and run snort is `Snort -l c:\snort\log -c C:\snort\etc\snoft.conf -A console`.

An IDS can perform either signature analysis or anomaly detection to determine if the traffic is a possible attack. Signature detection IDSs match traffic with known signatures and patterns of misuse. A *signature* is a pattern used to identify either a single packet or a series of packets that, when combined, execute an attack. An IDS that employs anomaly detection looks for intrusion attempts based on a person's normal business patterns and alerts when there is an anomaly in the behavior of access to systems, files, logins, and so on.

A hacker can evade an IDS by changing the traffic so that it does not match a known signature. This may involve using a different protocol such as UDP instead of TCP or HTTP instead of ICMP to deliver an attack. Additionally, a hacker can break an attack up into several smaller packets to pass through an IDS but when reassembled at the receiving station will result in a compromise of the system. This is known as session splicing. Some other methods of evading detection involve inserting extra data, obfuscating addresses or data by using encryption, or desynchronizing and taking over a current client's session.

Hacking Tool

ADMutate takes an attack script and creates a different—but functionally equivalent—script to perform the attack. The new script isn't in the database of known attack signatures and therefore can bypass the IDS.

List the Firewall Types and Honeypot Evasion Techniques

A *firewall* is a software program or hardware appliance that allows or denies access to a network and follows rules set by an administrator to direct where packets are allowed to go on the network. A *perimeter hardware firewall* appliance is set up either at the network edge where a trusted network connects to an untrusted network, such as the Internet, or between networks. A *software firewall* protects a personal computer, a system, or a host from unwanted or malicious packets entering the network interface card (NIC) from the network.

A *honeypot* is a decoy box residing inside your network Demilitarized Zone (DMZ), set up by a security professional to trap or aid in locating hackers, or to draw them away from the real target system. The honeypot is a decoy system that a malicious attacker might try to attack; software on the system can log information about the attacker such as IP address. This information can be used to try and locate the attacker either during or after the attack. The best location for a honeypot is in front of the firewall on the DMZ, making it very attractive to hackers. A honeypot with a static address looks just like a real production server.

The easiest way to bypass a firewall is to compromise a system on the trusted or internal side of the firewall. The compromised system can then connect through the firewall, from the trusted to the untrusted side, to the hacker's system. A common method of doing this is to make the compromised system connect to the hacker with destination port 80, which looks just like a web client connecting to a web server through the firewall. This is referred to as a *reverse WWW shell*.

This attack works because most firewalls permit outgoing connections to be made to port 80 by default.

Using a tunnel to send HTTP traffic, the hacker bypasses the firewall and makes the attack look innocuous to the firewall; such attacks are virtually untraceable by system administrators. Hacking programs can create covert channels, which let the attack traffic travel down an allowed path such as an Internet Control Message Protocol (ICMP) ping request or reply. Another method of utilizing a covert channel tunnels the attack traffic as a TCP acknowledgment.

To evade the trap set by a honeypot a hacker can run an anti-honeypot software that tries to determine whether a honeypot is running on the target system and warn the hacker about it. In this way a hacker can attempt to evade detection by not attacking a honeypot. Most anti-honeypot software checks the software running on the system against a known list of honeypots such as honeyd.

Hacking Tools

007 Shell is a shell-tunneling program that lets a hacker use a covert channel for the attack and thus bypass firewall rules.

ICMP Shell is a program similar to Telnet that a hacker uses to make a connection to a target system using just ICMP commands, which are usually allowed through a firewall.

AckCmd is a client/server program that communicates using only TCP ACK packets, which can usually pass through a firewall.

Covert_TCP is a program that a hacker uses to send a file through a firewall one byte at a time by hiding the data in the IP header.

Send-Safe Honeypot Hunter is a honeypot-detection tool that checks against a proxy server for honeypots.

Countermeasures

Specter is a honeypot system that can automatically capture information about a hacker's machine while they're attacking the system.

Honeyd is an open source honeypot that creates virtual hosts on a network that is then targeted by hackers.

KFSensor is a host-based IDS that acts as a honeypot and can simulate virtual services and Trojan installations.

Sobek is a data-capturing honeypot tool that captures an attacker's keystrokes.

Nessus Vulnerability Scanner (http://www.nessus.org/) can also be used to detect honeypots.

Exam Essentials

Know the two main types of IDSs.   IDSs can be either host-based or network-based. A host-based IDS is operating system–specific and protects a single system. A network-based IDS can protect the entire network.

Know the definition of a honeypot.   A honeypot resides in a DMZ as a vulnerable host and advertises services and software to entice a hacker to hack the system.

Know the definition of a firewall.   A firewall is a packet-filtering device that compares traffic to a list of rules and filters traffic from an untrusted network to a trusted network.

Understand how to detect a honeypot.   A honeypot can be detected by comparing the system information to to a known list of honeypots in a proxy server.

Understand how an IDS works.   An IDS can either perform anomaly analysis or signature-based detection.

Know how to perform firewall evasion techniques   Firewall evasion can be performed by using a protocol such as ICMP or HTTP to carry attack traffic. Another technique is to split the packets into several smaller packets so the entire attack string cannot be detected.

Review Questions

1. A system that performs attack recognition and alerting for a network is what?

   A. HIDS

   B. NIDS

   C. Anomaly detection HIDS

   D. Signature-based NIDS

2. Which of the following tools bypasses a firewall by sending one byte at a time in the IP header?

   A. Honeyd

   B. Nessus

   C. Covert_TCP

   D. 007 shell

   E. TCP to IP hide

3. Which of the following is a honeypot-detection tool?

   A. Honeyd

   B. Specter

   C. KFSensor

   D. Sobek

4. Which of the following is a system designed to attract and identify hackers?

   A. Honeypot

   B. Firewall

   C. Honeytrap

   D. IDS

5. Which of the following is a tool used to modify an attack script to bypass an IDS's signature detection?

   A. ADMutate

   B. Script mutate

   C. Snort

   D. Specter

6. What is a reverse WWW shell?

   A. A web server making a reverse connection to a firewall

   B. A web client making a connection to a hacker through the firewall

   C. A web server connecting to a web client through the firewall

   D. A hacker connecting to a web server through a firewall

7. A reverse WWW shell connects to which port on a hacker's system?

    A. 80

    B. 443

    C. 23

    D. 21

8. What is the command to install and run Snort?

    A. `snort -l c:\snort\log -c C:\snort\etc\snoft.conf -A console`

    B. `snort -c C:\snort\etc\snoft.conf -A console`

    C. `snort -c C:\snort\etc\snoft.conf console`

    D. `snort -l c:\snort\log -c -A`

9. What type of program is Snort?

    A. NIDS

    B. Sniffer, HIDS, and traffic-logging tool

    C. Sniffer and HIDS

    D. NIDS and sniffer

10. What are the ways in which an IDS is able to detect intrusion attempts? (Choose all that apply.)

    A. Signature detection

    B. Anomaly detection

    C. Traffic identification

    D. Protocol analysis

Answers to Review Questions

1. B. A NIDS performs attack recognition for an entire network.

2. C. Covert_TCP passes through a firewall by sending one byte at a time of a file in the IP header.

3. D. Sobek is a honeypot-detection tool.

4. A. A honeypot is a system designed to attract and identify hackers.

5. A. ADMutate is a tool used to modify an attack script to bypass an IDS's signature detection.

6. B. A reverse WWW shell occurs when a compromised web client makes a connection back to a hacker's computer and is able to pass through a firewall.

7. A. The hacker's system, which is acting as a web server, uses port 80.

8. A. `snort -l c:\snort\log -c C:\snort\etc\snoft.conf -A console` is the command to install and run the Snort program.

9. B. Snort is a sniffer, HIDS, and traffic-logging tool

10. B, C. Signature analysis and anomaly detection are the ways an IDS detects instruction attempts.

Chapter

14

Cryptography

CEH EXAM OBJECTIVES COVERED IN THIS CHAPTER:

- ✓ Overview of Cryptography and Encryption Techniques
- ✓ Describe How Public and Private Keys Are Generated
- ✓ Overview of MD5, SHA, RC4, RC5, Blowfish Algorithms

Cryptography is the study of encryption and encryption algorithms. In a practical sense, encryption is the conversion of messages from a comprehensible form (clear text) into an incomprehensible one (cipher text), and back again. The purpose of encryption is to render data unreadable by interceptors or eavesdroppers who do not know the secret of how to decrypt the message. Encryption attempts to ensure secrecy in communications. Cryptography defines the techniques used in encryption. This chapter will discuss encryption algorithms and cryptography.

Overview of Cryptography and Encryption Techniques

Encryption can be used to encrypt data while it is in transit or while it's stored on a hard drive. Cryptography is the study of protecting information by mathematically scrambling the data so it cannot be deciphered without knowledge of the mathematical formula used to encrypt it. This mathematical formula is known as the encryption algorithm.

Encryption algorithms can use simple methods of scrambling characters, such as *substitution* (replacing characters with other characters) and *transposition* (changing the order of characters). *Encryption algorithms* are mathematical calculations based on substitution and transposition. The two primary types of encryption are symmetric and asymmetric key encryption.

Symmetric key encryption means both sender and receiver use the same secret key to encrypt and decrypt the data. The drawback to symmetric key encryption is there is no secure way to share the key between multiple systems. Systems that use symmetric key encryption need to use an offline method to transfer the keys from one system to another. This is not practical in a large environment such as the Internet, where the clients and server could be on opposite sides of the world.

Asymmetric (or public) key cryptography was created to address the weaknesses of symmetric key management and distribution. Asymmetric key encryption will be covered in the next section of this chapter.

Describe How Public and Private Keys Are Generated

When a client and a server use asymmetric cryptography, both create their own pairs of keys for a total of four keys: the server's public key, the server's private key, the client's public key, and the client's private key. A system's key pair has a mathematical relationship that allows data encrypted with one of the keys to be decrypted with the other key. These keys have a mathematical relationship based on factoring prime numbers such that each key can be used to decrypt data encrypted with the other key. When a client and a server want to mutually authenticate and share information, they each send their own public key to the remote system, but never share their private keys. Each message is encrypted with the receiver's public key. Only the receiver's private key can decrypt the message.

The server would encrypt a message to the client using the client's public key. The only key that can decrypt the message is held by the client, which ensures confidentiality.

Overview of the MD5, SHA, RC4, RC5, and Blowfish Algorithms

Algorithms vary in key length from 40 bits to 448 bits. The longer the key length, the stronger the encryption algorithm. To brute-force crack a key of 40 bits ranges from 1.4 minutes to .2 seconds, depending on the strength of the processing computer. In comparison, a 64-bit key requires between 50 years and 37 days to break, again depending on the speed of the processor. Currently, any key with a length over 256 bits is considered uncrackable.

Message Digest 5 (MD5), Secure Hash Algorithm (SHA), RC4, RC5, and Blowfish are all names for different mathematical algorithms used for encryption. As a CEH, you need to be familiar with these algorithms:

MD5 MD5 is a hashing algorithm that uses a random-length input to generate a 128-bit digest. It is popular to create a digital signature to accompany documents and e-mails to prove the integrity of the source. The digital signature process involves the creation of an MD5 message digest of the document, which is then encrypted by the sender's private key. MD5 message digests are encrypted by a private key in the digital signature process.

SHA SHA is also a message digest, which generates a 160-bit digest of encrypted data. SHA takes slightly longer than MD5 and is considered a stronger encryption. It is the preferred algorithm for use by the government.

RC4 and RC5 RC4 is a symmetric key algorithm and is a *streaming cipher*, meaning one bit is encrypted at a time. It uses random mathematical permutations and a variable key size. RC5 is the next generation algorithm: It uses a variable block size and variable key size. RC5 has been broken with key sizes smaller than 256.

Blowfish   Blowfish is a 64-bit block cipher, which means that it encrypts data in chunks or blocks. It is stronger than a stream cipher and has a variable key length between 32 and 448 bits.

Exam Essentials

Understand the two types of encryption.   Symmetric key and asymmetric key encryption are the two main types of encryption.

Understand the methods used to scramble data during encryption.   Substitution and transposition methods are the basis of encryption and are used to scramble data during the encryption process.

Know the common encryption algorithms.   MD5, SHA, RC4, RC5, and Blowfish are the most common encryption algorithms.

Know how public and private keys are created.   A public key and a private key are created simultaneously as a key pair and are used to encrypt and decrypt data. Data encrypted with one member of the key pair can only be decrypted by the other.

Know the definition of cryptography.   Cryptography is the process of encrypting data through a mathematical process of scrambling data known as an encryption algorithm.

Review Questions

1. How many keys exist is in a public/private key pair?

    A. 1

    B. 2

    C. 3

    D. 4

2. How many keys are needed for symmetric key encryption?

    A. 1

    B. 2

    C. 3

    D. 4

3. Which of the following key lengths would be considered uncrackable? (Choose all that apply.)

    A. 512

    B. 256

    C. 128

    D. 64

4. What algorithm outputs a 128-bit message digest regardless of the length of the input?

    A. SHA

    B. MD5

    C. RC4

    D. RC6

5. What algorithm outputs a 160-bit key with variable-length input?

    A. SHA

    B. MD5

    C. RC4

    D. RC6

6. Which algorithm is used in the digital signature process?

    A. RC4

    B. RC5

    C. Blowfish

    D. MD5

7.   What is cryptography?

   A. The study of computer science

   B. The study of mathematics

   C. The study of encryption

   D. The creation of encryption algorithms

8.   What is the process of replacing some characters with others in an encryption key?

   A. Transposition

   B. Subtraction

   C. Substitution

   D. Transrelation

9.   Data encrypted with the server's public key can be decrypted with which key?

   A. Server's public key

   B. Server's private key

   C. Client's public key

   D. Client's private key

10. Which type of encryption is the fastest to use for large amounts of data?

   A. Symmetric

   B. Public

   C. Private

   D. Asymmetric

Answers to Review Questions

1.   B. Two keys, a public key and a private key, exist in a key pair.

2.   A. The same key is used to encrypt and decrypt the data with symmetric key encryption.

3.   A, B. A key length of 256 bits or more is considered uncrackable.

4.   B. MD5 outputs a 128-bit digest with variable-length input.

5.   A. SHA outputs a 160-bit key with variable-length input.

6.   D. MD5 is used in the digital signature process.

7.   C. Cryptography is the study of encryption.

8.   C. Substitution is the process of replacing some characters with others.

9.   B. Data can be decrypted with the other key in the pair—in this case, the server's private key.

10.   A. Symmetric key encryption is fast and best to use for large amounts of data.

Chapter

15

Penetration Testing Methodologies

CEH EXAM OBJECTIVES COVERED IN THIS CHAPTER:

- ✓ Defining Security Assessments
- ✓ Overview of Penetration Testing Methodologies
- ✓ List the Penetration Testing Steps
- ✓ Overview of the Pen-Test Legal Framework
- ✓ List the Automated Penetration Testing Tools
- ✓ Overview of the Pen-Test Deliverables

A penetration test simulates methods that intruders use to gain unauthorized access to an organization's network and systems and to compromise them. The purpose of a penetration test is to test the security implementations and security policy of an organization: basically to see if the organization has implemented security measures as specified in the security policy.

A hacker whose intent is to gain unauthorized access to an organization's network is very different from a professional penetration tester who lacks malice and intent and uses their skills to improve an organization's network security without causing a loss of service or a disruption to the business.

In this chapter, we'll look at the aspects of penetration testing (pen testing) that you must know as a CEH.

Defining Security Assessments

A penetration tester assesses the security posture of the organization as a whole to reveal the potential consequences of a real attacker compromising a network or application. Security assessments can be categorized as security audits, vulnerability assessments, or penetration testing. Each security assessment requires that the people conducting the assessment have different skills based on the scope of the assessment.

A security audit and a vulnerability assessment scan IP networks and hosts for known security weaknesses with tools designed to locate live systems, enumerate users, and identify operating systems and applications, looking for common security configuration mistakes and vulnerabilities.

A vulnerability or security assessment only identifies the potential vulnerabilities while a pen test actually tries to gain access to the network. An example of a security assessment is looking at a door and thinking if that door is unlocked it could allow someone to gain unauthorized access, whereas a pen test actually tries to open the door to see where it leads. A pen test is usually a better indication of the weaknesses of the network or systems but is more invasive and therefore had more potential to cause disruption to network service.

Overview of Penetration Testing Methodologies

There are two types of security assessments: external and internal assessments. An *external assessment* tests and analyzes publicly available information, conducts network scanning and enumeration, and runs exploits from outside the network perimeter, usually via the Internet. An *internal assessment* is performed on the network from within the organization, with the tester acting either as an employee with some access to the network or as a black hat with no knowledge of the environment.

A black-hat penetration test usually involves a higher risk of encountering unexpected problems. The team is advised to make contingency plans in order to effectively utilize time and resources.

You can outsource your penetration test if you don't have qualified or experienced testers or if you're required to perform a specific assessment to meet audit requirements such as the Health Insurance Portability and Accountability Act (HIPAA).

An organization employing an assessment term must specify the scope of the assessment, including what is to be tested and what is not to be tested. For example, a pen test may be a targeted test limited to the first 10 systems in a Demilitarized Zone (DMZ) or a comprehensive assessment uncovering as many vulnerabilities as possible. In the scope of work, a service-level agreement (SLA) should be defined to determine any actions that will be taken in the event of a serious service disruption.

Other terms for engaging an assessment team can specify a desired code of conduct, the procedures to be followed, and the interaction or lack or interaction between the organization and the testing team.

A security assessment or pen test can be performed manually with several different tools, usually freeware or shareware. A different approach is to use a more expensive automated tool. Assessing the security posture of your organization using a manual test is sometimes a better option than just using an automated tool based on a standard template. The company can benefit from the expertise of an experienced professional who analyzes the information. While the automated approach may be faster and easier, something may be missed during the audit. However, a manual approach requires planning, scheduling, and diligent documentation.

List the Penetration Testing Steps

Penetration testing includes three phases:

- Pre-attack phase
- Attack phase
- Post-attack phase

The *pre-attack phase* involves reconnaissance or data gathering. This is the first step for a pen tester. Gathering data from Whois, DNS, and network scanning can help you map a target network and provide valuable information regarding the operating system and applications running on the systems. The pen test involves locating the IP block and using domain name Whois to find personnel contact information, as well as enumerating information about hosts that can then be used to create a detailed network diagram and identify targets. You should also test network filtering devices to look for legitimate traffic, stress-test proxy servers, and check for default installation of firewalls to ensure that default users IDs, passwords, and guest passwords have been disabled or changed and no remote login is allowed.

Next is the *attack phase*, and during the attack phase tools can range from exploitive to responsive. They're used by professional hackers to monitor and test the security of systems and the network. These activities include but aren't limited to:

Penetrating the perimeter   This includes looking at error reports, checking Access Control Lists by forging responses with crafted packets, and evaluating protocol filtering rules by using various protocols such as SSH, FTP, and Telnet. The tester should also test for buffer overflows, SQL injections, bad input validation, output sanitization, and DoS attacks. In addition to software testing, you should allocate time to test internal web applications and wireless configurations, because the insider threat is the greatest security threat today.

Acquiring the target   This set of activities is more intrusive and challenging than a vulnerability scan or audit. You can use an automated exploit tool like CORE IMPACT or attempt to access the system through legitimate information obtained from social engineering. This activity also includes testing the enforcement of the security policy, brute-force password crackers, or the use of get admin tools to gain greater access to protected resources.

Escalating privileges   Once a user account has been acquired the tester can attempt to give the user account more privileges or rights to systems on the network. Many hacking tools are able to exploit a vulnerability in a system and create a new user account with administrator privileges.

Executing, implanting, and retracting   This is the final phase of testing. Your hacking skills are challenged by escalating privileges on a system or network while not disrupting business processes. *Leaving a mark* can show where you were able to gain greater access to protected resources. Many companies don't want you to leave marks or execute arbitrary code, and such limitations are identified and agreed upon prior to starting your test.

The *post-attack* phase involves restoring the system to normal pre-test configurations, which includes removing files, cleaning registry entries if vulnerabilities were created, and removing shares and connections.

Finally, you analyze all the results and presenting them in a comprehensive report and a report for management. These reports include your objectives, your observations, all activities undertaken, and the results of test activities, and may recommend fixes for vulnerabilities.

Overview of the Pen-Test Legal Framework

A penetration tester must be aware of the legal ramifications of hacking a network, even in an ethical manner. The laws applicable to hacking were discussed in Chapter 1 of this book. The documents that an ethical hacker performing a penetration test must have signed with the client are as follows:

- Scope of work, to identify what is to be tested
- Nondisclosure agreement, in case the tester sees confidential information
- Liability release, releasing the ethical hacker from any actions or disruption of service caused by the pen test

List the Automated Penetration Testing Tools

A 2006 survey of the hackers mailing list created a top-10 list of vulnerability scanning tools; more than 3,000 people responded. Fyodor (`http://insecure.org/fyodor/`), which created the list, says, "Anyone in the security field would be well advised to go over the list and investigate tools they are unfamiliar with." The following should be considered the top pen testing tools in a hacker's toolkit:

Nessus   This freeware network vulnerability scanner has more than 11,000 plug-ins available. It includes remote and local security checks, a client/server architecture with a GTK graphical interface, and an embedded scripting language for writing your own plug-ins or understanding the existing ones.

GFI LANguard   This is a commercial network security scanner for Windows. It scans IP networks to detect what machines are running. It can determine the host operating system, what applications are running, what Windows service packs are installed, whether any security patches are missing, and more.

Retina   This is a commercial vulnerability assessment scanner by eEye. Like Nessus, Retina scans all the hosts on a network and reports on any vulnerabilities found.

CORE IMPACT   CORE IMPACT is an automated pen testing product that is widely considered to be the most powerful exploitation tool available (it's also very costly). It has a large, regularly updated database of professional exploits. Among its features, it can exploit one machine and then establish an encrypted tunnel through that machine to reach and exploit other machines.

ISS Internet Scanner   This is an application-level vulnerability assessment. Internet Scanner can identify more than 1,300 types of networked devices on your network, including desktops, servers, routers/switches, firewalls, security devices, and application routers.

X-Scan   X-Scan is a general multithreaded plug-in-supported network vulnerability scanner. It can detect service types, remote operating system types and versions, and weak usernames and passwords.

SARA   Security Auditor's Research Assistant (SARA) is a vulnerability assessment tool derived from the System Administrator Tool for Analyzing Networks (SATAN) scanner. Updates are typically released twice a month.

QualysGuard   This is a web-based vulnerability scanner. Users can securely access QualysGuard through an easy-to-use web interface. It features more than 5,000 vulnerability checks, as well as an inference-based scanning engine.

SAINT   Security Administrator's Integrated Network Tool (SAINT) is a commercial vulnerability assessment tool.

MBSA   Microsoft Baseline Security Analyzer (MBSA) is built on the Windows Update Agent and Microsoft Update infrastructure. It ensures consistency with other Microsoft products and, on average, scans more than 3 million computers each week.

In addition to this list, you should be familiar with the following vulnerability exploitation tools:

Metasploit Framework This is an open-source software product used to develop, test, and use exploit code.

Canvas Canvas is a commercial vulnerability exploitation tool. It includes more than 150 exploits.

Overview of the Pen-Test Deliverables

The main deliverable at the end of a penetration test is the pen testing report. The report should include the following:

- List of your findings, in order of highest risk
- Analysis of your findings
- Conclusion or explanation of your findings
- Remediation measures for your findings
- Log files from tools that provide supporting evidence of your findings
- Executive summary of the organization's security posture
- Name of the tester and the date testing occurred
- Any positive findings or good security implementations

Exam Essentials

Know the definition of a security assessment. A security assessment is a test that uses hacking tools to determine an organization's security posture.

Know pen testing deliverables. A pen testing report of the findings of the penetration test should include suggestions to improve security, positive findings, and log files.

Know the legal requirements of a pen test. A pen tester should have the client sign a liability release, a scope of work, and a nondisclosure agreement.

List the penetration testing steps. Pre-attack, attack, and post-attack are the three phases of pen testing.

Know the two types of security assessments. Security assessments can be performed either internally or externally.

Review Questions

1. What is the purpose of a pen test?
    A. To simulate methods that intruders take to gain escalated privileges
    B. To see if you can get confidential network data
    C. To test the security posture and policies and procedures of an organization
    D. To get passwords

2. Security assessment categories include which of the following? (Choose all that apply.)
    A. White-hat assessments
    B. Vulnerability assessments
    C. Penetration testing
    D. Security audits
    E. Black-hat assessments

3. What type of testing is the best option for an organization that can benefit from the experience of a security professional?
    A. Automated testing tools
    B. White-hat and black-hat testing
    C. Manual testing
    D. Automated testing

4. Which type of audit tests the security implementation and access controls in an organization?
    A. A firewall test
    B. A penetration test
    C. An asset audit
    D. A systems audit

5. What is the objective of ethical hacking from the hacker's prospective?
    A. Determine the security posture of the organization.
    B. Find and penetrate invalid parameters.
    C. Find and steal available system resources.
    D. Leave marks on the network to prove they gained access.

6. What is the first step of a pen test?
    A. Create a map of the network by scanning.
    B. Locate the remote access connections to the network.
    C. Sign a scope of work, NDA, and liability release document with the client.
    D. Perform a physical security audit to ensure the physical site is secure.

7. Which tools are not essential in a pen tester's toolbox?

   A. Password crackers

   B. Port scanning tools

   C. Vulnerability scanning tools

   D. Web testing tools

   E. Database assessment tools

   F. None of the above

8. What are not the results to be expected from a pre-attack passive reconnaissance phase? (Choose all that apply.)

   A. Directory mapping

   B. Competitive intelligence gathering

   C. Asset classification

   D. Acquiring the target

   E. Product/service offerings

   F. Executing, implanting, and retracting

   G. Social engineering

9. Once the target has been acquired, what is the next step for a company that wants to confirm the vulnerability was exploited? (Choose all that apply.)

   A. Use tools that will exploit a vulnerability and leave a mark.

   B. Create a report that tells management where the vulnerability exists.

   C. Escalate privileges on a vulnerable system.

   D. Execute a command on a vulnerable system to communicate to another system on the network and leave a mark.

10. An assessment report for management may include suggested fixes or corrective measures.

   A. True

   B. False

Answers to Review Questions

1. C. A penetration test is designed to test the overall security posture of an organization and to see if it responds according to the security policies.

2. B, C, D. Security assessments can be security audits, vulnerability assessments, or penetration testing.

3. C. Manual testing is best, because knowledgeable security professionals can plan, test designs, and do diligent documentation to capture test results.

4. B. A penetration test produces a report of findings on the security posture of an organization.

5. A. An ethical hacker is trying to determine the security posture of the organization.

6. C. The first step of a pen test should always be to have the client sign a scope of work, NDA, and liability release document.

7. F. All these tools must be used to discover vulnerabilities in an effective security assessment.

8. D, F. Acquiring the target and executing, implanting, and retracting are part of the active reconnaissance pre-attack phase.

9. A, D. The next step after target acquisition is to use tools that will exploit a vulnerability and leave a mark or execute a command on a vulnerable system to communicate to another system on the network and leave a mark.

10. A. An assessment may include corrective suggestions to fix the vulnerability.

Glossary

Access Control List (ACL)   A table that maintains a detailed list of permissions or access rights granted to users or groups with respect to file directory, individual file, or network resource access.

access point (AP)   A piece of wireless communications hardware that creates a central point of wireless connectivity.

active attack   An attack that can be detected and is therefore said to leave a footprint.

Active Directory (AD)   A directory that stores information about resources on the network and provides a means of centrally organizing, managing, and controlling access to those resources.

Address Resolution Protocol (ARP)   A TCP/IP protocol used to resolve a node's physical address from a provided IP address.

agent   A software routine that performs designated functions, such as waiting in the background and performing an action when a specified event occurs.

anonymizer   A website that allows a user to access other website undetected by a proxy server.

anonymous   Having no known name, identity, or source.

anti-Trojan   Software specifically designed to help detect and remove Trojans.

antivirus   A program that attempts to recognize, prevent, and remove computer viruses and other malicious software from the computer.

archive   A place or collection containing records, documents, or other materials of historical interest.

auditing   Checking a computer system to verify intended programs and reliable data and to see whether the data is corrupted or displaying inaccurate results.

backdoor   A gap in the security of a computer system that's purposely left open to permit access. Hackers can create backdoors to a system once it has been compromised.

black-box testing   Testing a system or network without any knowledge of the internal structure.

banner grabbing   A technique that enables a hacker to identify the type of operating system or application running on a target server. A specific request for the banner is often allowed through firewalls because it uses legitimate connection requests such as Telnet.

Black hat   A malicious hacker.

buffer   A portion of memory available to store data.

buffer overflow   A situation where a program writes data beyond the buffer space allocated in memory. This can result in other valid memory being overwritten. Buffer overflows can occur as a consequence of bugs, improper configuration, and lack of bounds checking when receiving program input.

bug   A software or hardware error that triggers the malfunction of a particular program.

cache   A fast storage buffer, such as that found directly on the central processing unit of a computer.

calling procedure   A software routine that passes control to a different software routine. When these routines exist on separate computers, the systems often use Remote Procedure Call (RPC) libraries. Also refers to function calls and subroutines.

certificate authority (CA)   The organization or program that issues digital certificates.

Common Internet File System/Server Message Block   The standard for file sharing used with Microsoft Windows and IBM OS/2 operating systems.

client   A system or software process that accesses a remote service on another computer.

countermeasure   An action taken to offset another action. Usually a fix for a vulnerability in a system.

covert channel   A channel that transfers communication in a nonstandard way, often such that it can't be easily detected. Too frequently, this form of communication violates the security policy by using a channel in an unintended manner.

cross-site scripting   A computer security exploit that is used to execute a malicious script.

daemon   A background program that resides on a computer and services requests.

database   A collection of data or information that's organized for easy access and analysis.

decryption   The process of converting encrypted data to plain text.

Demilitarized Zone (DMZ)   A network area that sits between an organization's internal network and an external network, usually the Internet. Most publicly available servers such as Web and FTP reside in the DMZ.

digital certificate   Credentials that contain personal information such as a name, a public key, an expiration date, and the digital signature of the certificate authority that issued the certificate.

digital signature   A hash of a message that has been encrypted with an individual's private key. It serves as validation of a message's authenticity.

DNS enumeration   Locating DNS records from a DNS server.

domain name   A unique name that identifies a company or organization on the Internet.

Domain Name System (DNS)   The name resolution system that translates alphabetic domain names into numeric IP addresses.

encryption   The process of encoding information in an attempt to make it secure from unauthorized access.

enumeration   The creation of a list or inventory of items.

Ethernet   A frame-based computer networking technology for LANs. It defines wiring and signaling for the physical layer, frame formats, and protocols for the media access control (MAC) and data link layer of the OSI model.

exploit   A defined procedure or program that takes advantage of a security hole in a computer program.

Extended Stack Pointer (ESP)   A location identifier used to access parameters passed into a subroutine as arguments.

Fiber Distributed Data Interface (FDDI)   A standard for data transmission in a LAN.

File Allocation Table (FAT)   A filesystem used in DOS, Windows, and OS/2. It keeps track of where data is stored on disk.

firewalking   A method to collect information about a remote network protected by a firewall. Firewalking uses trace route–like IP packet analysis to determine whether a data packet can pass through the packet-filtering device/firewall from the attacker's host to the victim's host.

firewall   Rules created to enforce an Access Control List (ACL) and designed to prevent unauthorized access to or from a private network.

footprinting   Gathering information about a target to identify weaknesses.

fragmentation   The means of breaking a larger message into smaller chunks for the purpose of sending or storing the data more efficiently.

FreeBSD   A free, open source operating system based on Unix.

File Transfer Protocol SSL   A secure form of FTP software in which Secure Sockets Layer / Transport Layer Security (SSL/TLS) protocols are used to secure the control and data connections.

gateway   Software or hardware capable of decision-making, which permits or denies access based on general rules. Firewalls are layer 3 and layer 4 gateways.

GET   An HTTP command used to request a file from a web server.

Grey hat   A hacker who uses skills for defensive or offensive purposes as necessary.

hacktivism   Hacking for a cause.

hash   A function that transforms a string of characters into a number known as the *message digest*.

Hierarchical File System (HFS)   A filesystem used in Mac OS X. It stores data in a top-to-bottom organization structure.

honeynet   An entire virtual network that is presented as a large honeypot.

honeypot   A system that is designed to attract probes, attacks, and potential exploits. Because honeypots attract attacks, they can be a liability. However, by having honeypots on the network, you can gain enormous amounts of information about how a malicious hacker, or even a script kiddie, gains access to systems. This information can lead to security improvements and/or help a security professional track down a hacker.

hybrid attack   A password attack that combines features of a brute force attack with a dictionary attack. Characteristics of a hybrid attack include using dictionary terms that substitute numbers or special characters for letters or append numbers to words.

HyperText Transfer Protocol (HTTP)   A communication protocol that facilitates browsing the World Wide Web.

HyperText Transport Protocol Secure (HTTPS)   A secure version of the HTTP protocol used to access secure web servers.

Institute of Electrical and Electronics Engineers (IEEE)   An organization (sometimes referred to as the I Triple E) that creates standards that assist with the advancement of society's use of technology. It includes engineers, scientists, and students.

Internet Control Message Protocol (ICMP)   An encapsulated IP packet that is used to send error and control messages. The `ping` command uses ICMP echo requests and ICMP echo responses to verify connectivity.

Internet Protocol Security Architecture (IPSec)   A layer 3 protocol that provides secure tunneled communication with authentication and encryption over the Internet. It's often used to create a virtual private network.

intrusion detection system (IDS)   A mechanism to monitor packets passing through computer networks. The IDS can be monitored as a security check on all transactions that take place into and out of a system.

iris scanner   A biometric device containing a small camera that examines the iris of the eye for purposes of authetication.

Kerberos   A computer network authentication protocol.

keylogger   A software or hardware device that records information typed by users. Data is saved in a log file, which could be retrieved by a hacker.

Lightweight Directory Access Protocol (LDAP)   A protocol used to access simple directory structures.

local area network (LAN)   An in-house network made up of system nodes and peripherals.

logic bomb   A program with a delayed payload that is released only when certain conditions are met in the system or program environment.

malicious   Deliberately harmful.

mantrap   A secured entrance, normally reserved for high-security facilities. The trap usually involves a series of doors that someone must pass through and in which a trespasser could be detained by locking the doors.

Multipurpose Internet Mail Extensions (MIME)   A communication protocol that allows for the transmission of data in many forms, such as audio, binary, or video in e-mail messages.

NetBSD   The first freely redistributable, open source version of the BSD Unix operating system.

Network Address Translation (NAT)   A technique of mapping multiple IP addresses to a single external IP address belonging to the NAT device. This method is frequently used to connect multiple computers to the Internet.

Network Basic Input/Output System (NetBIOS)   An interface that provides communication between a PC and the network. It was created by IBM and adopted by Microsoft. NetBIOS includes a name service, a session service, and a datagram service.

network interface card (NIC)   A layer 1 and layer 2 device that provides upper-layer communication to a physical medium or medium type. Also known as a *network adapter*.

network scanning   Enumerating the available live hosts or IP addresses on a network.

NOP   A command that tells the processor to do nothing. Almost all processors have a NOP instruction that performs a null operation. In the Intel architecture, the NOP instruction is one byte long and translates to 0x90 in machine code. A long run of NOP instructions is called a *NOP slide* or *sled*. The CPU does nothing until it gets back to the main event (which precedes the return pointer).

NT LAN Manager (NTLM)   A challenge/response authentication protocol used in a variety of Microsoft network protocols for authentication purposes.

null session   An unauthenticated connection to a network share by an anonymous user on an unidentified system.

Open Systems Interconnection (OSI)   A standard created by the International Organization for Standards (ISO) that describes seven layers with distinct responsibilities in moving data as it's exchanged between two networked devices.

OpenBSD   An open source UNIX based operating system that has many available security measures.

overt channel   An obvious and defined communication path within a computer system or network, used for the transfer of data.

passive attack   An attack that violates the security of a system without directly interacting with the system.

password cracker   A program designed to decode passwords.

patch   A short set of instructions to correct a vulnerability in a computer program.

Personal Identification Number (PIN)   An alphanumeric value often used as a secondary form of identification when using two-form authentication.

phraselist   A list of passphrases that a password-cracking tool uses to attempt to crack a password.

physical security   Nondigital methods and mechanisms in place to prevent attackers from getting access to a facility, resource, or information stored on physical media. It can be a simple locked door or as elaborate as multiple security layers including armed guards.

ping   A common connection verification tool that uses ICMP messages to test a target's response. It's been nicknamed the Packet InterNet Groper.

ping sweep   A scan of a range of IP addresses that shows which IP addresses are in use and which aren't. Ping sweeps may include retrieving the DNS name for each live IP address.

Point-to-Point Protocol (PPP)   A protocol used for transporting IP packets over a serial link between the user and ISP.

policy   A set of rules and regulations specified by an organization as a basis for behavior, operation, or performance.

port scanning   Trying to identify the services running on a system by probing ports and viewing the responses from the system. This technique can be used to find services that indicate a weakness in the computer or network device.

POST   An HTTP command used to send text to a web server for processing.

Post Office Protocol 3 (POP3)   A standard interface for retrieving mail by an e-mail client program and from an e-mail server.

Pretty Good Privacy (PGP)   A software package that provides cryptographic routines for e-mail and file-storage applications.

private key   Half of the formula to perform public key cryptography. It's used to create a digital signature and to decrypt data that has been encrypted with the corresponding public key.

probing   Investigating or examining thoroughly.

process   An entity that is uniquely identifiable as it executes in memory.

protocol   A convention or standard that controls and enables communications, connections, and data transfers.

proxy server   A system that acts on behalf of other systems. Proxy servers are often focal points of a network and contain firewalls.

public key   Half of the formula to perform public key cryptography. Messages that have been encrypted with someone's public key can only be decrypted by the person's private key.

remote access   A communication method that allows access to a system or network from a remote location via a telephone line or the Internet.

Request for Comments (RFC)   A solicitation for professional discussion on a topic of interest. RFCs are often released when developing standards for protocols, systems, or procedures used by the Internet community.

rootkit   A collection of tools utilized by an intruder after gaining access to a computer system. These tools assist the attackers in any number of malicious purposes. Rootkits have been developed for all common operating systems, including Linux, Solaris, and Windows.

script   A text file containing ordered commands that a user can perform interactively at the keyboard.

Secure Hash Algorithm (SHA)   A cryptographic message digest algorithm, similar to the message digest family of hash functions developed by Ron Rivest.

Secure Shell (SSH)   Software that produces a secure logon for Windows and Unix using layer 7 of the OSI model.

Security Accounts Manager (SAM)   A database of usernames, passwords, and permissions in the Windows architecture.

security token   A small physical device used in multifactor authentication that can store cryptographic keys and /or biometric data for identity verification.

Sendmail   An SMTP implementation used in Unix.

Serial Line IP (SLIP)   A communications protocol for dial-up access to TCP/IP networks. It's commonly used to gain access to the Internet as well as to provide dial-up access between LANs.

server   A computer system in a network that provides services to client applications and/or computers.

Server Message Block (SMB)   A protocol for sharing files, printers, serial ports, and communications abstractions such as named pipes and mail slots between computers.

session   An active communication between a user and the system or between two computers. It also refers to layer 5 (the session layer) of the OSI model.

sheep dip   A stand-alone computer that houses antivirus software and is used under strictly controlled norms to check all media devices before they're connected to a network.

shell   A command language interpreter that is an interface between an operating system kernel and a user.

shellcode   Assembler code that can interact with the operating system and then exit. Hackers often use shellcode to launch exploits, such as stack-based overflows.

shredding   The physical destruction of the platters of a hard disk to ensure that the contents can never be recovered.

Simple Mail Transfer Protocol (SMTP)   A network protocol used when sending e-mail.

Simple Network Management Protocol (SNMP)   An application layer protocol that facilitates the set or read management information in the Management Information Base (MIB) of a network device.

Simple Object Access Protocol (SOAP)   A protocol for exchanging XML-based messages using HTTP or SMTP as the transport.

smart card   A device with an embedded microprocessor and storage space, often used with an access code to permit certificate-based authentication.

social engineering   The art of exploiting weaknesses common in human nature to trick a person into revealing useful information such as a user ID, password, or other confidential information.

spyware   Malicious software intended to intervene in or monitor the use of a computer without the user's permission. Spyware doesn't self-replicate like worms and Trojans.

steganography   The practice of hiding a message within an image, audio, or video file. It's a form of a covert channel.

System Integrity Verifier (SIV)   A program that monitors system file hashes to determine whether a file has been changed, such as if an intruder altered or overwrote a system file. Tripwire is one of the most popular SIVs.

TCP/IP   The protocol suite of definitions for communications at layers 3 and 4 of the OSI model. TCP/IP is the standard communication method that computers use to communicate over the Internet.

Telnet   An application used to create a remote session with a computer.

Temporal Key Integrity Protocol (TKIP)   An encryption standard defined in IEEE 802.11i and WPA for Wi-Fi networks designed to replace WEP. TKIP was structured to replace WEP with a more secure solution without replacing legacy hardware.

third party   A person, group, or business indirectly involved in a transaction or other relationship between principals.

threat   An intentional or unintentional action that has the capability of causing harm to an information system.

time bomb   A type of logic bomb, with a delayed payload that is triggered by reaching some preset time, either once or periodically.

time to live (TTL)   A field in the IP header that indicates the amount of time a transmitted packet will be valid. The TTL defines how many router hops a packet can make before it must be discarded. If a packet is discarded by a router, an ICMP error message is generated to the sender.

timestamp   A number that represents the date and time. Recording timestamps is important for tracking events as they occur on a computer.

Token Ring   A LAN protocol that resides at the data link layer (Layer 2) of the OSI model. It uses a token passing access method and connects up to 255 nodes in a star topology at 4, 16, or 100 Mbps.

traceroute   A tool to trace a path to a destination system.

traffic   The data being transferred across the network media.

Trojan horse   A program that seems to be useful or harmless but in fact contains hidden code embedded to take advantage of or damage the computer on which it's run.

tunneling   Encapsulating one protocol or session inside the data structure of another protocol.

tunneling virus   A virus that attempts to tunnel underneath antivirus software so that it's not detected.

Uniform Resource Locator (URL)   The address that defines the route to a file on a web server (HTTP server).

User Datagram Protocol (UDP)   The connectionless, unreliable Internet protocol that functions at layer 4 of the OSI model.

virus   Malicious code written with an intention to damage the user's computer. Viruses are parasitic and attach to other files or boot sectors. They need the movement of a file to infect other computers.

virus hoax   A bluff in the name of a virus. Creators attempt to arouse fear, and sometimes encourage the removal of system files.

virus signature   A unique string of bits that forms a recognizable binary pattern. This pattern is a fingerprint that can be used to detect and eradicate viruses.

vulnerability   A bug or glitch in computer software, an operating system, or architecture that can be exploited, leading to a system compromise.

vulnerability scanning   Searching for devices, processes, or configurations on your network that have known vulnerabilities.

war dialer   A malicious application that randomly calls phone numbers while trying to detect the response of a computer modem.

warchalking   A technique to identify key features of Wi-Fi networks for others by drawing symbols in public places (where anyone can intrude easily) and encourage open access.

web server   The computer that delivers web pages to browsers and other files to applications via the HTTP protocol.

web spider   Scanning web sites for certain information such as e-mail accounts.

white-box testing   Testing software, a system, or a network with knowledge of the internal structure. Also called *glass box testing*.

Wi-Fi   A certification from the Wi-Fi alliance to promote interoperability of wireless equipment for 802.11 networks (including 802.11b, 802.11a, 802.11g, and 802.11n). This term was popularized by the Wi-Fi Alliance.

Wired Equivalent Privacy (WEP)   A technically obsolete protocol for wireless local area networks (WLAN). WEP was proposed to present a level of security similar to that of a wired LAN.

wiretapping   A process by which a third party intervenes in a telephone conversation, usually through a secret medium.

worm   A malicious software application that is structured to spread through computer networks. These applications are self-propagating.

Index

Note to the Reader: Throughout this index **boldfaced** page numbers indicate primary discussions of a topic. *Italicized* page numbers indicate illustrations.

C

Q

R

S

The Best CEH Quick Reference Book/CD Combo Available!

Brush up on key Certified Ethical Hacker topics with hundreds of challenging review questions!

- Two bonus exams available only on the CD. Each question includes a detailed explanation.

- Glossary of Key Terms for instant reference.

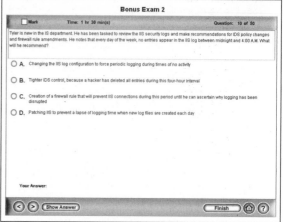

Use the Glossary of Terms for instance reference!

- Focus on the important topics and zero in on the term you need to know to pass the exam.

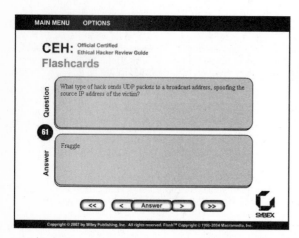

Reinforce understanding of key topics with flashcards for your PC, Pocket PC, or Palm handheld!

- Contains over 100 flashcard questions.

- Runs on multiple platforms for usability and portability.

- Quiz yourself anytime, anywhere!

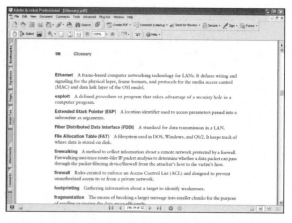